Denis A. Quinn

## Heroes and Heroines of Memphis

Reminiscences of the yellow fever epidemics that afflicted the city of Memphis during the autumn months of 1873, 1878 and 1879

Denis A. Quinn

**Heroes and Heroines of Memphis**
*Reminiscences of the yellow fever epidemics that afflicted the city of Memphis during the autumn months of 1873, 1878 and 1879*

ISBN/EAN: 9783337196295

Printed in Europe, USA, Canada, Australia, Japan

Cover: Foto ©ninafisch / pixelio.de

More available books at **www.hansebooks.com**

# Heroes and Heroines of Memphis,

OR

# REMINISCENCES

OF THE

YELLOW FEVER EPIDEMICS THAT AFFLICTED THE
CITY OF MEMPHIS DURING THE AUTUMN
MONTHS OF 1873, 1878, AND 1879,

TO WHICH IS ADDED

A GRAPHIC DESCRIPTION OF MISSIONARY LIFE IN
EASTERN ARKANSAS,

BY REV. D. A. QUINN.

---

*Quaeque ipse miserrima vidi,*
*"Et quorum pars magna fui."*
    *Virgil, Aeneis II.*

---

PROVIDENCE, R. I.
E. L. FREEMAN & SON, STATE PRINTERS.
1887.

TO

# His Grace, Most Rev. P. A. Feehan,

FORMER BISHOP OF NASHVILLE, PRESENT ARCHBISHOP OF

CHICAGO,

THE EVER-FAITHFUL, FEARLESS, AND TRUE SERVANT OF GOD,

THE VERITABLE "CAPTAIN" OF THE MARTYR-HEROES

OF MEMPHIS,

WITH THE HEART-FELT WISH THAT GOD MAY PROLONG

HIS YEARS, AND INSURE HIS HAPPINESS

HERE, AND HEREAFTER,

THIS LITTLE VOLUME

IS MOST RESPECTFULLY INSCRIBED.

# PREFACE.

Seeing that the History of Yellow Fever,* written soon after the panic of 1878, was so "sparing" of catholic facts that it scarcely referred to Catholicism, I expected then, and during the past seven years never resigned the hope, that some clergyman of the diocese of Nashville, or worthy catholic citizen of Memphis, more competent than myself, would write an impartial History of the Lives of those Martyr-Heroes and Heroines, who, in imitation of their divine Master, "laid down their lives for the people."

As up to the present year no one appears to have undertaken this task, I considered it an act of justice to the memory of the "departed," as also a laudable exemplar of unflinching faith, to record my "Yellow-Fever Reminiscences."

In those instances where I have assumed a hilarious, when a serious tone would be more in keeping with the gravity of the subject, I simply meant to compensate for the many tearful events I had previously recorded, or had yet to record.

If my narration of facts and "tributes" to the "departed" are not couched in grandiloquent words, or choice diction, I have only to regret that some one more capable than myself has not appropriated the subject.

However, as all men have to acknowledge some little repertory of self-complacency, or self-conceit, I, too, have mine.

Apart from the pleasure it affords me to extol the virtues of my "departed" comrades, I feel assured that, as there are thousands yet living in Tennessee who can attest the facts I indite, my little book will be read, if not with admiration, at least with interest and pleasure.

REV. D. A. QUINN,<br>
BAY-VIEW SEMINARY,<br>
PROVIDENCE, R. I.

*February* 25, 1887.

* By Hon. J. M. Keating.

PRIESTS' MONUMENT, CALVARY CEMETERY, MEMPHIS.

[Except Nos. 22, 23 and 24, all the Priests whose names are mentioned in the opposite page are buried around this monument.]

# Obituary.

### PRIESTS.

| | NAME. | DIED. | AGED. |
|---|---|---|---|
| 1. | Rev. J. R. DAILY, O. P. | Sept. 23, 1873 | 27 |
| 2. | Rev. B. V. CARY, O. P. | Oct. 7, 1873 | 40 |
| 3. | Rev. D. A. O'BRIEN, O. P. | Oct. 9, 1873 | 42 |
| 4. | Rev. J. D. SHEEHY, O. P. | Oct. 17, 1873 | 43 |
| 5. | Rev. FATHER LEO, O. S. F. | Oct. 17, 1873 | 45 |
| 6. | Rev. MARTIN WALSH | Aug. 29, 1878 | 40 |
| 7. | Rev. J. A. BOKEL, O. P. | Aug. 29, 1878 | 29 |
| 8. | Rev. J. R McGARVEY, O. P. | Aug. 29, 1878 | 33 |
| 9. | Rev. MICHAEL MEAGHER | Aug. 30, 1878 | 46 |
| 10. | Rev. FATHER ERASMUS, O. S. F. | Aug. 31, 1878 | 30 |
| 11. | Rev. PATRICK McNAMARA | Sept 3, 1878 | 28 |
| 12. | Rev. V. P. MATERNUS, O. S. F. | Sept. 9, 1878 | 35 |
| 13. | Very Rev. MARTIN RIORDAN, V. G. | Sept. 17, 1878 | 50 |
| 14. | Rev. P. J. SCANLON, O. P. | Sept. 19, 1878 | 30 |
| 15. | Rev. V. B. VANTROOSTENBERG | Sept. 19, 1878 | 35 |
| 16. | Rev. JAMES J. MOONEY | Sept. 27, 1878 | 46 |
| 17. | Rev. German FATHER, O. S. F. | 1878 | |
| 18. | Rev. EDWARD DOYLE | Sept. 4, 1879 | 46 |
| 19. | Rev. JOHN FAHEY | Sept 6, 1879 | 29 |
| 20. | Rev. CHRYSOSTOM REINIKE, O. S. F. | Sept. 9, 1879 | 39 |
| 21. | Rev. D. E. REVILLE, O. P. | 1879 | 39 |
| 22. | Rev. PATRICK RYAN (Chattanooga) | 1878 | 38 |
| 23. | Rev. JOHN F. WALSH (small-pox) | Feb. 19, 1882 | 28 |
| 24. | Very Rev. JOSEPH A. KELLY, O. P. | Sept. 7, 1885 | 50 |

### NUNS.

Mother GERTRUDE, Superioress of Franciscan Convent; aged 41; died in 1873. ALPHONSA, Superioress, Good Shepherd Convent; aged 34; died in 1878. Sister ROSE, aged 30; 1878. Sister JOSEPHA, aged 44 years; 1878. Sister MARY BERNARDINE, aged 40 years; 1878. Sister MARY DOLORA, aged 24 years; 1878. Sister MARY VERONICA, aged 19 years; 1878. Sister WILHELMINA, aged 30 years; 1878. Sister VINCENT, aged 22 years; 1878. Sister STANISLAUS, aged 21 years; 1878. Sister GERTRUDE, aged 28 years; 1878. Sister WINKELMAN, 1878. Sister FRANCES, Sister CATHERINE, Sister VERONICA, and some thirty-five others.

### PRAYER.

Absolve, we beseech Thee, O Lord, the souls of thy servants here named, that, being dead to this world, they may live to Thee; and whatever sins they may have committed through human frailty, do Thou, of thy most merciful goodness, forgive, through Jesus Christ, our Lord. Amen.

*Requiescant in pace.*

# CORRIGENDA.

The foot-note at the end of page 1 gives the population of Memphis in 1880, 33,452; in page 12, line one, it is stated that the population was reduced to 31,000 in 1879, instead of 60,000 in '73; in page 139, the context gives 65,000 as the population in 1878. These discrepancies may be attributed either to the fluctuating decline or progress of Memphis, or the different statistics given by various authors. My own unbiassed opinion leads me to state that immediately before the Fever of '73, Memphis had a population averaging from 50,000 to 55,000, which number in '79 was reduced to about 33,000.

In page 38, line 5, read: *sandaled*, instead of *sandalled*.

Page 90, line 28, read: *cosmogony*, instead of *cosmogany*.

Page 129, first line of prose context, read: Virulency *of the* Fever, instead of Virulency Fever.

In page 139, line 12, read: Some eight hundred *went to the* Howard Encampment, instead of some eight hundred a Howard Encampment.

Page 143, read: Very Rev. M. Riordan, aged *50*, instead of *46*.

Page 169, line 11, read: *lætitia*, instead of *letitia*.

Page 178, line 13, read: *instil*, instead of *instill*.

Page 207, line 12, read: Victims *of* Cromwellian cruelty, instead of victims *of the*, &c.

Page 264, line 26, read: *run*, instead of *ran*.

# TESTIMONIALS.

CHICAGO, Jan. 28, 1887.

DEAR FATHER QUINN:—I am greatly pleased to learn that you are about to preserve from oblivion the memory of the heroic Priests and Religious of the diocese of Nashville who gave their lives during the Yellow Fever epidemics of 1873, '78 and '79. It is very befitting that you should record events of which you can truthfully say: "*Quorum pars magna fui.*" In the history of the church there will be no grander chapter than that which will narrate the noble devotion and self-sacrifice of our Priests and Sisters during those most trying times. Wishing you every success, I remain,

Sincerely and faithfully yours,

P. A. FEEHAN,
*Abp., Chicago.*

LITTLE ROCK, Feb. 4, 1887.

DEAR FR. QUINN:—With much pleasure I give you the statement you desire: that you were engaged in the Little Rock diocese from 1871 to 1878, and had charge of the Memphis & Little Rock Railroad Missions as far west as Brinkley, and of the whole Mississippi district fronting our State. Your book will, I am sure, furnish interesting reading for all who passed through the memorable Yellow Fever years of '73, '78 and '79.

Yours truly,

EDWARD FITZGERALD,
*Bp., Little Rock.*

DIOCESE OF NASHVILLE,
NASHVILLE, TENN., Feb. 15, 1887.

REV. DEAR FATHER QUINN:—Allow me to congratulate you on the noble work to which, as you inform me, you are devoting your leisure hours—to preserve the record of those true martyrs of Charity, the Priests and Religious who fell in Memphis, as victims of their zeal and devotion, in the Yellow Fever epidemics of 1873, '78 and '79.

X.   TESTIMONIALS.

Your labors, during these eventful years, in Memphis and the neighboring missions—Brownsville, Humboldt, Covington, Grand Junction, Milan and Mason; the close personal and social relations you thus formed with the subjects of your "Reminiscences," and the prominent part you took in the events you are to describe, qualify you in an exceptional manner for the work, and whilst enhancing its interest, guarantees its success and faithful execution.

I beg, moreover, to acknowledge with sincere thanks the service you are about to render the diocese of Nashville. You will discharge a debt of gratitude which she owes to the memory of her noblest children, whose sublime devotion to duty and heroic self-sacrifice shed such lustre upon her history. Hoping and praying that their spirit of Apostolic zeal and Charity may ever abide with us, and wishing you every blessing, I am, Rev. Dear Father,

Yours sincerely in Xto,

JOS. RADEMACHER,
*Bp., Nashville.*

---

EPISCOPAL RESIDENCE,
PROVIDENCE, R. I., March 8, 1887.

REV. D. A. QUINN:

REV. DEAR SIR:—I am pleased to learn that you propose to publish a book giving an account of your experience of the visitations of that dreadful scourge—Yellow Fever—in Memphis, Tennessee, in the years 1873, '78 and '79.

A truthful account of the sufferings of the people and fidelity of the Priests and Nuns, who displayed in an eminent degree the qualities of the Good Shepherd, whom the fear of death could not deter from the duties of their missions of love, will, no doubt, be read with interest, not only by the people of Memphis and the South, but by the people of the North and the Catholics of this diocese, of which you are so respected a subject. The deeds of heroism which you have witnessed, and in which you have taken an active part, while edifying the faithful, will glorify the church of God. Wishing you every success, I remain,

Yours very sincerely,

M. M. McCABE, *Adm.*, (*sede vacante*)
*Diocese of Providence.*

# CONTENTS.

|  | PAGE. |
|---|---|
| Memphis | 1 |
| Fatal Effects of Fever | 8 |
| What caused the Physical and Financial Decline of Memphis? | 11 |
| The Mississippi River | 19 |
| Explanatory Remarks | 25 |
| Rev. William Walsh | 30 |
| Very Rev. J. A. Kelly, O. P. | 34 |
| Rev. Aloysius Weiver, O. S. F. | 35 |
| Rev. P. O'Brien | 39 |
| Where the Fever was supposed to have Germinated | 42 |
| Churches and Educational Institutions of Memphis | 47 |
| Most Rev. P. A. Feehan | 51 |
| Condition of Memphis after the Fever of '73 | 54 |
| Rev. D. O'Brien, O. P. | 55 |
| Rev. V. B. Cary, O. P. | 56 |
| Rev. J. R. Daily, O. P. | 56 |
| Police and Firemen of Memphis | 58 |
| Fraternal and Benevolent Societies | 60 |
| Fatal Consequences of the Fever of '73 | 66 |
| Walthal Infirmary | 86 |
| Incidents of the Fever of '73 | 88 |
| Rev. J. D. Sheehy, O. P. | 102 |
| Dr. Luke Blackburne | 103 |
| Mattie Steveson | 114 |
| Undertaker Jack | 116 |
| The Yellow Fever Scourge of 1878 | 125 |
| The much-abused, but sensible Irishman, John D— | 134 |
| Camp Father Mathew | 139 |
| Priests who died of Fever in '78 | 142 |
| Rev. M. Meagher | 148 |
| Very Rev. M. Riordan, V. G. | 150 |
| Rev. M. Walsh | 156 |
| Rev. P. McNamara | 159 |

## CONTENTS.

|  | PAGE. |
|---|---|
| Rev. E. Doyle | 161 |
| Rev. J. J. Mooney | 165 |
| Rev. J. Fahey | 168 |
| Revs. Bokel, McGarvey, Reville, O. P. | 169 |
| Rev. P. Ryan | 171 |
| Catholic Sisterhood of Memphis | 175 |
| The Fever-Proof Band of St. Joseph Sisters | 182 |
| Incidents of the Fever of '78 | 185 |
| Thrilling Incidents | 195 |
| Extract from Keating's History | 200 |
| Some Outspoken Facts | 203 |
| General Remarks | 211 |
| Cities that escaped the Fever—Nashville | 220 |
| Right Rev. Jos. Rademacher | 227 |
| History of Yellow Fever | 230 |
| Synopsis of Missionary Life in Eastern Arkansas | 235 |
| A Priest's Missionary Valise | 236 |
| Hopefield, Marion and Mound City | 240 |
| Forest City, Brinkley and Osceola | 244 |
| An Arkansas Quagmire | 255 |
| The Little Rock Railroad | 257 |
| Inhabitants of the Swamps | 264 |
| Irish Immigrants in Eastern Arkansas | 266 |
| The Hoosier, or Country Native Arkansian | 271 |
| The Diocese and Bishop of Little Rock | 300 |
| An Apology | 305 |

# REMINISCENCES

#### OF THE

# Yellow Fever Epidemics of 1873, '78 and '79.

## MEMPHIS.*

The City of Memphis (at present called the "Taxing District" of Shelby County), situated on a pleasant "Bluff," whose western slope overhangs the Mississippi river (lat. 35.9, long. 90), includes within its corporation limits about eight square miles, being the product of its extreme length from Chelsea to Fort Pickering, four miles, north and south; and from the river-front to the intersection of Poplar and Dunlap streets, two miles, east and west.

Towards the commencement of the year 1873, Memphis had a population of some sixty thousand. Of these, about one-third belonged to the colored race, while the remaining two-thirds consisted (like other American cities) of white native born citi-

---

\* According to census of 1880 (Rand & McNally), the population of Memphis was 33,452.

zens and immigrants from Ireland, Germany, France and Italy. From its first settlement until the eventful year, '73, the increase of wealth and population in Memphis was unprecedented. At that period several Irish and German residents distinctly remembered when Memphis was but a village; when droves of cattle grazed upon the land, which then, as now, formed its chief thoroughfares.

### COURT SQUARE IN SUMMER.

To see Memphis in a "nut shell," the Northern tourist should enter that beautiful city "reservation" known as Court Square. From this impaled enclosure, the visitor can enjoy the beauties of both country and city life. On the green, daisy-bedecked sward, shaded by miniature forests of lilac, cypress, myrtle and cedar trees, moistened by the spray of its marble fountain, might be seen artistic flower beds, circumscribed by mimic walls of pinks, geraniums, violets and heliotropes. Blooming on either side of semi-circular promenades and pleasant avenues, was a choice variety of the two flower queens, the rose and lily, surrounded by a multitude of sweet-breathing honeysuckles, clover and buttercups. But to the Northern tourist there is nothing half so enchanting as the climatic mocking bird, poised on some leafy bough of the Southern native and incomparably fragrant "Magnolia."

It is very pleasant to watch another Southern native—the Humming bird, flitting about or burying his long beak and starry forehead in the moist bosom of a rose or peach blossom; but to feel a thrill of ravishing enjoyment, the Southern wild mocking bird must be heard with leisure:—

> "Winged mimic of the woods! thou motley fool,
> Who shall thy gay buffoonery describe?
> Thine ever-ready notes of ridicule
> Pursue thy fellows still with jest and jibe;
> Wit, Sophist, Songster, Yorick of thy tribe,
> Thou sportive satirist of Nature's school;
> To thee the palm of scoffing we ascribe,
> Arch-mocker and mad abbot of misrule!"
> — *Wilde.*

While reclining in the park, you see, here and there, the nurse, the baby and the baby carriage; the tired or glutted tramp, or, forsooth, the lover and his lady, sitting or strolling over the very spot where, ten years before, the portly hog wallowed in the sunshine, and the long-bearded "William" browsed or slept beside his more useful neighbors, the cow, the sheep and the mule.

Turning from the rural landscape to city life, we see, at no great distance, the large warehouses and wholesale business firms of Second street, facing the richly furnished dry goods stores, jewelry establishments and public offices of Main street.

On every adjacent street you hear the rumbling of numerous vehicles, from the humble hand and grocery-cart, dray and ice wagon to the more pretentious gurney, cab and horse-car. The fruit men and women are chanticleering the merits of their stock with a very sad tone in their screeching. On either sidewalk you behold man and womankind of every description: the chubby little daughter in "shorts" making love to her well dressed mamma in seal or silk, or perhaps trying to elicit her mamma's affection for a doll or a new hat; the gaunt country "hoosier" striding past his fashionable city brother, whose bosom front and gold mounted cane sparkle in the sunlight: the little newsboys and girls, singing out in various national tones, "*Appeal!* only five cents;" "*Avalanche!* all about the late 'scandal' in Fort Pickering," or the "'murder and robbery' on Wolf Creek." The evening *Ledger* leaves poor Catholic "*Adam*" far behind in the race for dollars and dimes.

The ill-requited bootblack is ever at your service in Court Square. "Shine your boots!" Lately they have prefixed a very enticing word to their "shining" capabilities: "Mister" or "Miss, won't you let me shine your nice little boots?" This irresistible appeal causes the loftiest notions of the Memphis belle to descend to her feet; even the gents can scarcely resist the temptation of admiring their "nice little boots."

If the tourist's visit to Court Square has been in the early morning, he cannot avoid hearing the cheery whoop of the street milkman, calling out the sleepy damsel of the kitchen, not in a plaintive semi-tone like the charcoal man's: nor a sad minor like the fruit woman's, "Char - coal! Char - coal!" nor the octave in which the anxious mother calls her truant boy, thus: but a wild, funny, unwritable howl, expressive "Jim - my!" at once of haste, good humor, and good understanding with the cook, who is to pop out from the rear entrance. If she does not come at once—and she seldom does, liking the "lordliness," perhaps, as well as her lady— the jolly milkman shouts once more, with the addition of "wide awake!" or "all alive, now!" or "come, my girl!" though this last is generally reserved till the papillated head comes in sight.

But it is time to bring the reader from the scenery of Court Square to the history of early Memphis.

1*

Speaking of early Memphis, some old citizens tell a story which, for all I can vouch, may be a very *fine* "yarn."

One fine morning during the "fall" of September, a country negro was seen leisurely driving his mule team loaded with cotton, the product of his year's toil, along that thoroughfare since macadamized Beale street. All of a sudden he and his mules sank into the earth. Some days after, a hat was discovered, partly concealed by the mud. The hat was found to rest upon a human head. After several hours' excavating, the cotton was unearthed, but the poor negro and his mules had already gone to that "bourne whence no 'white folk' or 'darkies' ever return." *

Although no such occurrence could take place in Beale or any other paved street in

---

\* The following is a clipping from a Memphis weekly, of date February 12, 1887:

One of the leading thoroughfares to the city is Johnson avenue. In the fall of last year that part of the bed of the road leading to Alabama street was dug up, and three or four feet of the surface given away to some wealthy lot owners. Citizens and tax-payers on the avenue petitioned the council for the grading of the avenue, from which crossings and grade levels for sidewalks were removed. The avenue was reported dangerous and almost impassable. No heed was paid to the remonstrances so frequently made. On last Saturday morning the milk wagon of J. T. Briggs was sent in, on its usual trip over the avenue, and in the early morn the cries of the driver were heard, as himself, wagon and horse were being absorbed in a vortex on the avenue. Forty gallons of milk were vainly sacrificed to the deity of the vortex, and a *few hours afterward* cables were anchored on the wagon to resurrect it. A number of men worked these cables until they succeeded in dragging the wagon ashore. Ike came along with his mule and made soundings, and reporting "no bottom!" The citizens on Johnson avenue are going to vote a medal to Pap. Hadden & Co.

Memphis to-day, still, it must be acknowledged that several roads leading to Memphis (Johnson's avenue, Old Raleigh, Pigeon Roost and Hernando Roads) are yet capable of ingloriously engorging a teamster to the waist and a team to the hubs.

I often witnessed country farmers tasking their wits as well as muscular energy, endeavoring to stimulate four strong mules to drag their empty teams as far as the city limits. Indeed, I would rather undertake a journey from Providence to Memphis than ride from the city poor-house to Estival Park in bad weather. The following clipping from *Adam*, a Memphis Catholic weekly, of Jan. 8, 1887, although evidently ludicrous, must have some pertinent cause for its insertion :

"President Hadden (acting Mayor) is in Nashville, arranging for a balloon in which he can visit some of the streets and avenues of Memphis during the next ninety days. A boss balloon, capable of buoying up a mule and a load of coal, is being prepared for the especial accommodation of coal men."

Of course, these difficulties occurred only in moist or rainy weather. The same can be said of all Southern and other cities where sand and rock are not indigenous.

I make these palliative remarks to obviate the insinuation that young and old Memphians of either sex must be a "terror" to palace-car porters, school janitors and sextons;

that while Nashvillians, their ancient rivals, tread upon sand and cobble, they are destined to love and pray, marry and get divorced in dirty boots. There is provision made for such emergencies. Instead of burying their dainty feet in pasty mud, the fair and less fair "sex" envelop them in rubber "Wellingtons." Memphis, when out of her "rubbers," has an upper and lower understanding, as solid and "polished" as any city in the land.

### FATAL EFFECTS OF FEVER IN MEMPHIS.

Returning to the prosperous year, '73, it was a pleasant reminiscence for real estate owners, that the land and lots they purchased ten or fifteen years before, for so many cents a square rood, they could now sell for several hundred dollars a lineal foot.

One instance of a purchase made in the year 1866 will convey an idea of the enormous value of property at the time; while its subsequent depreciation will show what a calamitous effect Yellow Fever had, not only on human life, but also on real estate.

Very Rev. M. Riordan, Vicar General of the diocese of Nashville, purchased a cemetery site three and a half miles outside the city limits. The price he paid for eighty acres ($40,000) was considered a great bargain at the time. The unpaid principal was to bear interest at the exorbitant rate of ten per cent. Apart the sacred character of the land, what was it actually worth after the panic of '78? I doubt if a business man in Memphis would take a mortgage on it for four thousand dollars. Further, if it were not that these grounds held "those" that were dear and sacred to the Catholics of Memphis, the land was scarcely worth the cost of reclamation. And yet, the man who sold this land to the Catholics (making no allowance for the decrease in value) relentlessly demanded his "pound of flesh." After the Fever had subsided, there was still some amount over nine thousand dollars due on the cemetery. The agent of the sale said, "A bargain is a bargain. We must have the last cent of our money."* More than the first principal was already paid over in exorbitant interest at the time.

Seeing that money was not forthcoming, the agent's lawyer caused a fence to be built right through the centre of the mound wherein lay the bodies of twenty-two martyr priests, who died for the people. In sight of this vandalism, the once proud Catholics of Memphis held down their heads in sorrow. Rest-

* $9,137.13 due F. M. White, agent of Kerr estate; $4,000 due Butchers and Drovers' Bank, St. Louis; $5,000 due J. G. Elder; $5,444.32 due Emmet Bank, Memphis; $4,000 due Memphis Insurance Co.

ing beneath the adjacent willows, were the remains of brave Irishmen, who, if living, would never tolerate a rude fence post within a few inches of a Martyr's bones.

By these scathing remarks, I do not wish to throw all the odium on the agent of the sale. I suppose he simply did what he considered his duty. I can only say it was sad the Catholics were so scanted in their store of "savings" that they were unable to anticipate this shameful crisis.

I trust I will not overtask the reader's patience when I repeat that if there is a venerable spot in America, it is that "hallowed mound" that contains the "remains" of so many young and resolute Martyrs. The rose, tulip and lily that bloom outside might well envy the happy lot of their lovely companions within this sacred plot. Far and wide through the States, and across the ocean in Ireland, faded leaves, plucked from those graves, are kept in fond memory.

While Father Riordan lived, he did all in his power to meet the ever-flowing tide of interest; and had Memphis continued to progress, he might have lived to see his church and cemetery out of debt. But when some of his best people died in '73, he was forced to invest the church money and every available fund to satisfy the cemetery corporation.

This unfortunate purchase not only involved St. Patrick's (of which Father Riordan was pastor), but St. Bridget's and St. Peter's churches were to some extent compromised. In order to meet the creditors' demands, the cemetery directors were forced to make laws, some of which were stringent and odious. If a pauper's grave were to be given, the application that he was penniless should have the pastor's signature. It was forbidden to bring the corpse in a hearse or have a carriage accompanying. In several cases Catholics who had spent their reserved funds during the Fever found it impossible to purchase lots at the price demanded.

The Bishop of the diocese, Right Rev. P. A. Feehan, sanctioned the issue of "Calvary cemetery bonds" to aid those poor creditors who lent money to Father Riordan in his financial difficulties. I can vouch the good Bishop, from his own private resources, paid several large sums of money to appease anxious creditors.

### WHAT CAUSED THE PHYSICAL AND FINANCIAL DECLINE OF MEMPHIS?

Ever since the year 1873, the growth of Memphis ceased, or rather it continued to decline until '79, when its population was reduced to thirty-one thousand (instead of sixty thousand in '73). What primary cause can be assigned for this alarming decrease? It is not the geographical situation of Memphis. In this respect Memphis possesses decided advantages. For "shipping" and "receiving," it is the most accessible; and for the needy planter, it is the most feasible cotton mart between St. Louis and New Orleans; while it is the most direct centre for emigration to Arkansas, Texas, and the great West. To what, then, shall we ascribe the decline of Memphis? As I have already insinuated, I do not hesitate to state Yellow Fever has been the cause. "Yellow Jack," as it sometimes enjoys the sobriquet, has been the "bane and curse," not only of Memphis proper, but of all the towns one hundred miles above and two hundred miles below the city, on the Mississippi river. As the chief city of a great State, Memphis had reason to rejoice at the facilities that made her depots and harbor the outlets to commerce and emigration. But a city destined to flourish, needs, besides a central place in the map of the States, a favorable topography. With all due respect to the citizens and property owners of Memphis, to whom it is a question of dollars and cents to depreciate their fair city, I beg to state that, in this latter respect, Memphians have little or no reason to congratulate themselves. Right opposite Memphis, with nothing but the river dividing, you see the great forests and swamps of Arkansas. During the spring and autumn, these swamps are covered with a sheet of stagnant water inland to the St. Francis river, a distance of 40 miles, and along the confines of the Mississippi, from New Madrid to Helena, a distance of 200 miles. I specify these limits, not that the swamps do not extend far beyond, but in so far as they bear upon the history and health of Memphis. To thoroughly understand the location of Memphis, it is further necessary to state that a considerable portion of Tennessee, and that part of the State of Mississippi in the vicinage of Memphis, are also swampy and unarable. Take, for instance, Jackson, which is the nearest important town to Memphis. It is nothing but an oasis in the midst of a loathsome quagmire. Then, right under the shadow of Memphis, in Mississippi, pretty little Hernando has always the chills and fever. Tennessee has, towards the south, quite a number of other pretty little village daughters, who, if they have not the "ague," are going to have it soon.

I would be wishing well to my friends in Brownsville, Humboldt, Bolivar and Grand Junction, if I prayed they should never be obliged to take a more bitter "dose" than this flimsy sarcasm. If those noble philanthropists, Messrs. Holbrook and Keely, were living, they would endorse this description. And there is, at my writing this, a man *still* living in Grand Junction (McLaughlin) who has the terrors of Yellow Fever in his heart.

It is generally allowed that Yellow Fever is not indigenous to Memphis. Grant the "spore" is exotic. What is this when it vegetates with such alarming rapidity? The bones of twenty thousand men, women and precious little children, now sleeping in Elmwood and Calvary Cemeteries, prove the last assertion. Whether the prime germ is a creeping plant or an invisible animalcule, it has poisoned the best flesh and blood of Memphis. I am not prepared to give a fixed opinion as to the cause of Yellow Fever in Memphis. In fact, people living a thousand miles distant can furnish, in this regard, as reliable information as the inhabitants themselves. Even when a patient is afflicted with the Fever, it is almost impossible to diagnose its presence. I believe few clergymen or physicians in Memphis have seen more cases of Yellow Fever than myself. Outside an epidemic, I could not certify as to its existence. Some of the most eminent physicians of Memphis assured me that, were they to see in a Northern city a person having the supposed symptons, they would banter the notion of Yellow Fever. It commences with a light or a severe chill. Then a fever follows, which may or may not be checked, and still the patient dies. There is no special color or visible mark to indicate the presence of a foreign distemper. I grant that, in most cases, there is great thirst; but then there are others that have no thirst, and you cannot be sure which is the better sign. A Priest in '78 told me he could always detect the presence of Fever by an offensive odor as he passed the house in which it was. It reminded him, he said, of decayed flesh or of an old nest of rats. I experienced the same odor, but I always attributed it to excessive perspiration or bedding not properly aired. But what about black vomit? This, I allow, appears to be an invariable sign wherever it occurred; but then, as a warning, this comes too late to afford an opportunity to relieve the patient. Besides, I knew several persons who died without retching.

Physicians may say this is all nonsense. "We can diagnose as well as locate the existence of Yellow Fever." In reply, I can positively vouch that almost every physician whose opinion I asked concerning patients was invariably mistaken in the result. Those whom they distinctly asserted would succumb, survived; while those whom they designated as *sure* to live were *sure* to die. Besides, not a few of those good men indited a very different "prescription" for their own wives and children at home. It was a simple and, I must allow, a most efficient homœopathic remedy — "Pack your Saratogas and make ready to decamp as soon as possible." Many a skilful family physician might be seen playing marbles or "blind man's buff" with his little boys and girls 500 miles away, while his enamelled shingle and office hours in Memphis wafted to the breeze during the eventful autumn of '78. I am not disposed to censure them for this. If christian charity "begins at home," it is only fair to allow the Doctor to save himself and his family first. Although it appears a streak of jocularity, it is an incontestable fact that those physicians who "ran away" saved far more than those who remained.

Lest my remarks should create a hostile impression, I beg to state, in justice to the medical fraternity of Memphis, that as a body they can compare with their brethren in any city of the Union. Some of the most successful and skilful physicians in America, I do not hesitate to say, are to be found in

## DECLINE OF MEMPHIS. 17

Memphis. The late Doctors Rice, Cavenagh and Taylor, if they had equals, had no superiors in their profession. If Northern physicians claimed superior science, they not only failed to exhibit it, but showed a lack of ambition by not volunteering to heal poor prostrate Memphis.

The "spores" or "germs" of Fever not only deceived the physicians of Memphis, but heretofore have baffled human research. The people simply know it comes. That is all.

The next question, How or why does fever spread? If we accept the opinions of certain wiseacres, who attribute its propagation to foul air or defective sewerage, in this, also, we are left in a hopeless quandary. It is worthy of mention that since the year 1879, when the city was thoroughly flushed and sewered, no case of Fever has since occurred in Memphis. But this fact does not speak for Chattanooga (300 miles distant), nor for the other towns of Tennessee and Mississippi that were ravaged by the Fever of '78. The citizens had no compulsory sewerage in Brownsville, Humboldt, Milan or Covington, yet these places have escaped since '79, just as Memphis. I have no faith myself in the theory that drainage pipes, sewers, and other domestic precautionary experiments can ever place Memphis beyond the reach of Yellow Fever. If the Fever this or next year were to break out in Grenada, as it did in '78, I *firmly* believe Memphis could never guard against the infection.

It is my *firm* conviction that, until the Mississippi river is properly leveed, the miasmatic swamps of Arkansas, Mississippi and Missouri will always destine Memphis a fitting soil for the spread of this woful plague. And, granting that Yellow Fever does not re-visit Memphis every year, this immunity is no sign that in the meantime the surrounding swamps will fail to do their mischief.

During my residence of nine years in that ill-fated city, I regret to say that, compared to Northern or Eastern cities, Memphis has had more than an average share of malaria, chills and pneumonia. It cannot be expected otherwise in a city whose head is bathed in the murky waters of Wolf Creek, and flank and feet washed by the unfiltered waters of a fickle, but headstrong, river that submerges eight thousand square miles of adjacent country (40 by 200 miles). Although the inhabitants consider it healthy, you could scarcely see a red marble in a glass of Mississippi water. The sediment is either sand or mud; I mean when the water is fresh. To a fertile imagination, or under a microscope, there may be in it infinitesimal "protoplasms," that would upset the brain of another Darwin or Huxley. Not wishing to malign a river *no more* than an individual, I must say this mud is not proper to the Mississippi, but rather indigenous to the Missouri (mud river).

## THE MISSISSIPPI RIVER.

The waters of the Mississippi (Indian Miche Sepe, Father of Waters), from its source in Lake Itasca to its confluence with the Missouri, a few miles above St. Louis, are clear as crystal. In '72, I travelled from St. Paul, Minn., to St. Louis, and thence to New Orleans (2000 miles) by steamboat. Leaving St. Paul, you notice swivel metal bridges spanning the river at every important town until you reach St. Louis. Below this city, until you reach the Gulf of Mexico (1,250 miles), there is no stationary communication between the opposite States. As you pass Dubuque, Davenport, Burlington and Quincy, the waters are translucid, if not perfectly transparent. In all this distance, until you come to Alton, a few miles above St. Louis (where the Missouri meets the Mississippi), there is no "caving" of the river banks. From Alton, or rather from Cape Girardeau (50 miles below St. Louis), where both rivers commingle, all the way to New Orleans, the waters are noticeably opaque and murky. From this latter town we may also trace the immense tract of country inundated by the Mississippi and its tributaries, the Ohio, Arkansas, Red, White, Yazoo and St. Francis rivers. Viewing the country on either side of the river, from this town until you reach Memphis, and thence to New Orleans, the entire country, during the spring and fall, presents to the eye nothing but impenetrable forests of cedar, cypress, canebrake, and impassable swamps. The river flows in a serpentine course, slowly encroaching, if not engorging, on the east the levees fronting Columbus, Randolph, Memphis, Vicksburg, Natchez and Baton Rouge; while it attacks Helena on the west or opposite side. The river-bed is so irregular and tortuous that, from the mouth of the Ohio, at Cairo, to the Gulf, is 1,097 miles, whereas, by a straight line it is but six hundred miles. It sometimes forms almost a complete circle, as at Bayou Sara and Vicksburg, where a cut of one mile would shorten the route twenty-five miles. In the adjacent lakes, wild fowl, gar fish and alligators abound; while deer, panthers, wolves, bears and wild cat are frequently met in the forests. Although the Mississippi, from the "falls" of St. Anthony to the mouth of the Ohio, has an average depth of six feet, still, during certain parts of the year navigation in the Upper Mississippi is difficult, if not frequently very dangerous, owing to the presence of snags and sand bars. If sand bars (accumulated sand) do not always prove destructive, they never fail to be very annoying and tedious, delaying regular packets two and three hours, and sometimes as many days. A snag is the river-pilot's most dreaded spectre. As the decayed trunks or limbs of trees that have fallen in the river become imbedded in the sand, they present a formidable obstacle to the frail hulk or prow of a passing steamboat. Their presence, unlike the sand bar, can seldom (unless when exposed to view) be detected by the trained eye of the pilot.

To a stranger, it appears an insolvable problem how human vision, however observant, can steer the largest floating palace, as well as the smallest craft, through these pathless waters, beset by countless hidden dangers. It is safe to say that a salt water pilot would not steer a toy steamer displacing a depth of thirty inches, half a mile, on the Mississippi river, before he would be "stranded," "snagged," or "blown up." The alluvial lands on either side of the Mississippi, from Memphis to the Gulf, are indescribably rich. I have seen growing in the fields corn-stalks fifteen (15) and cotton twelve feet in height. The land can yield three plentiful crops in the year. Yet, within the next century there is little likelihood these regions will become the settled home of civilized man. So long as the Mississippi river is left to its wayward meandering course, the States that are invaded by its waters will neither be habitable nor healthy. To confine the river to its natural bed, and thus save the surrounding country, it would be necessary to construct an entirely new levee, from the mouth of the Ohio to the Gulf of Mexico (1,095 miles). It is not probable the Government will expend the enormous outlay necessary to complete this work for many years to come.

The "Century magazine" of March, 1883, thus describes the country bordering on the lower Mississippi:

"On the banks of these immense waters, surrounded by dikes, sluices and bayous, lie hundreds of miles of the richest plantations in America. The scenery of this land, where it is yet in its wild state, is weird and funereal; but on the banks of the large bayous, broad fields of corn, of cane, and of rice, open out at frequent intervals on either side of the stream, pushing back the dark, pall-like curtain of moss-draped swamp, and presenting to the passing eye the neat and often imposing residence of the planter, the white double row of field hands' cabins, the tall red chimney and broad gray roof of the gin-house. Even when the forests close in upon the banks of the river, there is a wild and solemn beauty in the shifting scene, which appeals to the imagination when the cool morning lights or the warmer glows of evening impart the colors of the atmosphere to the surrounding wilderness, and to the glassy waters of the narrow and tortuous bayous that move among its shadows. In the last hour of day, these scenes are often illuminated with an extraordinary splendor. From the boughs of the dark, broad spreading live-oak, and the phantom-like arms of lofty cypresses, the long, motionless pendants of pale gray moss point down to their inverted images in the unruffled waters beneath them. Nothing breaks the wide-spread silence. The light of the declining sun at one moment brightens the tops of the cypresses; at another, glows like a furnace behind their black branches, or broadens down in dazzling crimsons and purple upon the mirror of the stream. Now and then, from out some hazy shadow, a heron, white or blue, takes silent flight; an alligator crossing the stream sends out tinted bars of widening ripples; or on some high, fire-blackened tree a flock of roosting vultures, silhouetted on the sky, linger with half-opened, unwilling wing, and flap away by ones and twos until the tree is bare."

A great part of the country between Vicksburg and New Orleans is not only marshy and uninhabitable, but an impassable quagmire. For several miles above New Orleans you can see, as the train passes, the landscape, as far as the eye can reach, yielding like an earthquake to the weight of the train. For some twenty miles the railroad track is resting on spiles driven into the earth. I have often noticed plants, brushwood and even trees making suspicious, if not ominous, courtesies to the passing trains. When travelling by steamboat you would think it almost a pity to see every now and then exposed to view the great roots of some gigantic forest trees, that are soon to be buried in or carried away by the river.

As in this short chapter I have undertaken to give a brief description of the Mississippi, and the incalculable ruin it entails upon the Southern country, I do not wish to leave in the reader's mind a sinister impression of the river itself. It is truly a majestic stream, justly entitled the "Father of Rivers"; and if we compute the immense volume of waters which it annually pours into the ocean, is unquestionably the mightiest river on the surface of the globe.

I will pass on to another subject, as I quote the following lines from the poet Wordsworth:

> "Never did sun more beautifully steep
> In his first splendor, valley, rock or hill;
> Ne'er saw I, never felt, a calm so deep!
> The river glideth at his own sweet will.
> Dear God! the very houses seem asleep;
> And all that mighty heart is lying still."

### EXPLANATORY REMARKS.

While relating these "Reminiscences," I do not intend to assert or insinuate that I have been a great hero myself through all the plagues that visited the unfortunate city of Memphis. Those who deserve this distinction are supposed to have performed (what I never did) some extraordinary feats or valorous deeds. It appears to me almost impossible that a clergyman, bound to do what christian charity and the solemn duties of his office obliged, could deserve the title of hero at all. These remarks do not refer to those clergymen who volunteered their services, or who, being away, came to Memphis and dared the danger, in their zeal to save or assist the people. What enhances heroism, is the fact of its spontaneity and the absence of censure or disgrace in its non-performance. I must grant that a layman or cleric who risks his life for his fellow-man through pure motives of charity or philanthropy, may be reputed a hero, while the merits of the act would be common-place, were either forced by the requirements of duty.

By these remarks, I do not wish to belittle or depreciate the actions of those clergymen who had greater zeal and physical energy than I could display. If, in '73, circumstances obliged me to perform duties that were more than average, in '78 and '79, other Priests had to "bear the burden of the day and the heat." During these two years, I was not called upon to overtask my energies or risk my life like some of my brother clergymen. I happened then to have charge of "missions" in the country. Although I chose Memphis my place of residence (it being the most central), I had to attend missions more than two hundred miles distant, and scattered through four States—Tennessee, Arkansas, Mississippi and southern Missouri. In the two latter States, I attended only those missions that bordered on Tennessee or Arkansas.

During the prevalence of Yellow Fever in Memphis, quarantine regulations were so stringent that I found it in several instances impossible to attend to the spiritual wants of the people under my charge. No Priest or layman leaving an infected district (in fact, leaving any district) could enter another town or locality, unless he had a Doctor's or Board-of-Health certificate. All these precautions, however, did not prevent the Fever spreading through the country and rural villages. Some of the little towns and settlements in my charge were almost decimated. After attending a few stricken families in Paris, Tenn., (200) miles from Memphis) for several days I was regarded as an object of terror to Catholics as well as Protestants. After leaving Memphis and going to Covington, and afterwards to Brownsville, my presence in both places almost created a panic. Being heartily tired of this sort of isolation, I wrote to Rev. Martin Walsh (two days before he died), requesting him to let me take his place. Father William Walsh, his successor, took charge of this letter, which the person addressed never read. This letter, according to Rev. William Walsh, who returned it to me after the Fever, arrived too late, the Priest being too weak to read or act upon its contents.

Having received no reply from Memphis, I wrote to Bishop Feehan (from Clarksville), explaining to him my position, and expressing an unconditional willingness to go to Memphis or elsewhere at his direction. He answered by telegram, requiring me to go to Nashville immediately. I remained there over three weeks, when I started for Memphis. At this time, although the death-roll had considerably abated, the Fever had by no means subsided. After my return to Memphis, and for several weeks after the city withdrew quarantine precautions, I visited several families stricken with Fever. My predicament in '79, on account of the repetition of quarantine strictures, was not more encouraging. The act of a Priest attending one Yellow Fever patient was generally bruited for miles throughout the neighborhood. Seeing Catholics and Protestants equally afraid, a Priest felt loath to encroach where his absence was more desirable. Under feelings of such mortification, I addressed the Bishop, stating a preference to go to Memphis. The following is a copy of his reply:

NASHVILLE, 24th July, 1879.

DEAR FATHER QUINN:—I have just received your letter telling me of your readiness to go to any "post" of danger So far, all the Priests are well in Memphis, and you must not expose yourself unnecessarily. If a necessity arise, I will let you know. You had better stay in Clarksville for the present, or we would be glad to see you in Nashville.

Very faithfully yours,

P. A. FEEHAN, *Bp*.

After mentioning these facts, further detail is uncalled for. And, as I disclaim all pretensions to individual heroism, I trust the clergy and laity of Memphis will not dispute the only credit I wish to claim—that, whether in the city or the country, in common with the other Priests of the diocese, I did my duty to the best of my ability, and never deserted my post.

When the Fever of '78 broke out, I was taking a month's vacation in St. Louis with the Rev. Father Henry, of that city. I could, without risk of censure, remain away that entire summer, as quarantine regulations made it impossible for me to visit my missions; yet I preferred to return to Tennessee and outwit the vigilance of pickets and sanitary police, in order to render all the service I could to the suffering people. I never avoided or evaded a case of Yellow Fever, cholera, or small-pox, the breadth of a common sidewalk. I mention this not to "blow my own horn," but to state an indisputable fact. At all events, no one can say that, like some professional gentlemen, I ran away to play "ring taw" or "blind man's buff" during the epidemics. In this adherence to the place of duty, I feel honored to have belonged to that noble band of clergy who, while thousands fled to save their lives, remained with the few paupers and penniless patients who were unable to escape. All through the Fever of '78 the stroke of the executioner's axe or clasp of the guillotine did not appear more certain or fatal than exposure to one case of Fever. Not an individual Priest sent to Memphis during any of its Fevers escaped death. They were mostly all young, strong men, in the prime of life; men who, being religiously, physically, and intellectually my superiors, sad to think, were stricken down, while debilitated invalids were left to survive! Except myself and two others, there is no Priest living now who had witnessed the Fever of '73; while Fathers William Walsh, A. Luiselli, and Aloysius, O. S. F., are the only survivors of '78 and '79.

### REV. WILLIAM WALSH.

During the Fever of '78, the Rev. William Walsh, at present Rector of St. Bridget's church, Memphis, was most conspicuous in his appeals to the "Temperance Unions" and the country at large, soliciting aid towards the Yellow Fever sufferers. Although the Rev. gentleman did not seek printed notoriety, his position as President of the State Union, and chairman of the local Memphis lodge, made his name, or rather his fame, very remarkable. With all due deference to this gentleman's humility, I must, in justice, say that he did most efficient work during the two latter plagues that afflicted Memphis. Although from the peaceful town of Callan, county Kilkenny, he assumed martial airs and energy during these dreadful times. There were Generals, Captains, Colonels garrisoned at Camp Williams, who did not then, nor even in their best days, a fraction of the chivalrous work of Rev. Mr., or, as he showed the tactics, Rev. General Walsh, of Camp Mathew.

> "Dream not helm and harness
> The sign of valor true;
> Peace hath higher tests of manhood
> Than battle ever knew."
>
> —*The Hero, by Whittier.*

The notion of erecting a camp (something unknown to a majority of Priests), writing to the Secretary of War for tents, rations, army blankets, and biscuits, etc.; appealing to the Hierarchy, "Temperance Unions," and laity of America, I might say on his own responsibility, is entirely due to the zeal and fertile brain of Rev. W. Walsh. There may be some citizens who refuse to give credit to Father Walsh for all he did. Indeed, if there should be any such, they are ungrateful. I make bold to state there was not an Irishman in Memphis, at the time, possessed anything like his superior tact or diplomacy.

Although Camp Williams was almost entirely under Government patronage, its discipline and morale could stand no comparison with Camp Father Mathew. Even some of the pastors considered Father Walsh's notion of erecting a camp premature, if not Quixotic. In spite of all opposition, he carried out his scheme. And it is a superlative recommendation when I say he succeeded. He was here, there and everywhere, among the sufferers of '78 and '79. By his appeals to the "Temperance Unions" and Priesthood of America, he realized almost forty thousand dollars. He impartially divided this among the poor Catholics and Protestants, black and white. When the Fever was over, I remember being with him myself, distributing bags of silver. In less than two weeks we must have disbursed some eight thousand dollars to widows, orphans, and others who had suffered from the Fever. As in all similar cases, some were dissatisfied. But this was owing to the grudge of their own hearts, rather than the lack of generosity on the part of Father Walsh.

This young Priest, while visiting his aged parents in Ireland, in '79, hearing of the reappearance of the Yellow Fever in Memphis, after taking a hurried farewell of parents, brothers and sisters, embarked on the first ocean steamer bound for New York; and, having landed, took the first train for Memphis. As no trains were allowed into the city, I well remember the morning he chartered a locomotive to bring him from Grand Junction to Memphis, a distance of 52 miles. This young clergyman, having a leave of absence, was not bound to leave home and return to Memphis. He had acted well—*bravely* the year previous. He would incur no censure had he remained away during that summer. It is all well for a Priest to attend to his people while he is in their midst, but having gotten a prolonged leave of absence to recuperate his health, and being three thousand miles away, he could hardly be expected to rush into the open jaws of death. Father Walsh did this act of refined Christian Charity, if not veritable heroism.

In this panegyric, apparently biased in favor of Father Walsh, I have, by no means, forgotten two other remarkable Memphis Priests. One of these, Father Kelly, has been recently called to receive what the good Catholics of Memphis would gladly bestow upon him — an imperishable crown. The other clergyman, to whom I shall refer later on, is the Rev. Father Aloysius Weiver, O. S. F., Superior of the Franciscan Convent in Memphis.

## VERY REV. J. A. KELLY, O. P.

Joseph A. Kelly was born in the city of Dublin, and baptized in St. Michael's church of that city, in the year 1827. In his youth he was left without a mother. In company with his little sisters, he was brought to this country by his father, whose remains now repose at St. Rose, Ky. He was educated at St. Mary's, Bardstown, Ky.; completed his novitiate at St. Rose Convent, where he took his religious vows and became a professed member of the Order of Friar Preachers in the year 1850. He was ordained Priest by the late Archbishop Purcell. Ever since, he filled almost every office of trust and honor which the great Order of St. Dominic could confer. Before the arrival of Bishop Feehan, he was Administrator of the diocese of Nashville, subsequently pastor of St. Peter's church, Memphis, and once Provincial of the entire Dominican Order in this country.

This Priest was brought almost to the point of death by an attack of Yellow Fever in '73; he fought his way through all the plagues that invaded Memphis. In the darkest days of the Fever, it was always refreshing to meet Father Kelly. He was the soul of charity in word and act. He was never heard speak harshly of a neighbor, whilst he invariably defended the absent, even when they were avowedly hostile to himself or the church.

Being corpulent, and rather advanced in years, it was pitiful to see this heavy-gaited old man, sometimes during the darkest hours of night, climbing from cellar to attic, or making his way through lanes and alleys, sweltering from heat and fatigue. Although a man of profound knowledge and solid piety, he was most unassuming and ever cheerful. While other Priests recounted their ghastly day's work with a certain air of proud animation, Father Kelly would either smile or change the subject. Although this old Priest had himself witnessed most heart-rending, if not thrilling, scenes, yet he was too manly to mention or refer to them. Like another Eleazor, who refused to eat flesh which was lawful, but likely to cause suspicion, Father Kelly could not be induced to speak a light word or do a weak act. He died Aug. 7, 1885.*

May the many virtues he planted on earth bear fruit for him in Heaven; may the intercession of the countless orphans, to whom he was always a kind and indulgent father, obtain for him mercy, rest and peace.

### FATHER ALOYSIUS WEIVER, O. S. F.

Although personally acquainted with this Rev. gentleman for more than eight years, I

---

* His remains are buried beneath St. Peter's Church altar, Memphis.

regret my inability to furnish detailed facts of his life before he came to Memphis.

He was born in Germany, and was brought to this country while yet a mere child. He joined the "Order" of St. Francis, and received "Holy Orders" at the novitiate house in Joliet, Illinois, from which place he came to Memphis in 1873. At this time he did not appear more than twenty-four years of age.

He contracted a malignant type of Yellow Fever in '73, and was despaired of by Doctors and fellow-assistants. However, as soon as he was able to walk, he was seen again on the streets. He appeared like a gaunt spectre in the distance. His coarse habit, white cincture, and long beads, indicated what he really was, a veritable hermit.

At present I cannot say whether this good Father is living or dead. But this I can positively assert, he was a fearless man of God; and a true representative of St. Francis the founder of his "Order." Even when the Priests themselves took sick, it was Father Aloysius that was generally called to give them the last Sacraments.

As it has been said of the present Pope, Leo XIII, that no one ever regarded his countenance that did not associate him with the Saints in Heaven, so a glance at the pale repose of this Priest's lengthy features invariably convinced he was a living Saint. He simply knew nothing of the wiles and wicked ways of the world. His every word and act seemed to have immediate reference to the "business of his Eternal Father."

During the plagues of Memphis some Priests were especially mentioned, both in print and verbal report, as having attended large numbers of sick and dying, in fact, two or three were signalized as unique Heroes.

Having no desire to impugn the well-earned deserts of other clergymen who died or lived during this awful time, I make bold to state that Father Aloysius, in his own silent way, did more priestly work than any other clergyman of the diocese, living or dead. I feel that many will consider this assertion gratuitous. I have only to say that my experience and many years' residence in the same city force me to acknowledge this fact. If this Priest's name was seldom or never noticed in the papers, and no grand present or grateful testimonials offered to him, the fact only shows how blind the public eye can sometimes be, when there is a question of real merit.

Two or three Priests, (amongst whom was myself,) after the Fever, received magnificent gold watches, as testimonials for zeal or what the people called heroism. With all respect to those honored Priests, and strict honesty to myself, I feel constrained to avow that neither one of us had to encounter the hardships and exposure of this Priest. On his almost naked sandalled feet, he had to walk from house to house under the burning heat of the sun; his church being the most central, was most frequently visited; while he, himself, never left the city. Moreover the demeanor of this man gave the applicant to understand that besides a duty, it afforded him pleasure to attend a sick call.

This young Father was an acknowledged favorite. I remember once seeing him enter a crowded street car. A Protestant lady politely offered him the seat she occupied. On his refusal, as if by a united impulse, every lady and gentleman (most of them Protestants) stood up, and declared they would not resume their places until he would take the seat proffered him by the lady. A more saintly or resolute man I sincerely believe, never crossed the Ocean or left the German Fatherland.

With this exception, it would be hard to single out an individual Priest of Memphis, who outstripped his fellows in the exercise of zeal and christian charity. The Priests who died, as well as those who lived through the plagues did noble work, which has been recorded by a more remunerative pen than mine, and which, I trust the Father of Mercies will, hereafter, amply compensate.

## FATHER P. O'BRIEN.

(*Born in the Parish of Cahercomlish, Co. Limerick, Ireland.*)

The following account, taken from a Chicago Journal, of the life and labors of this clergyman is so concise and appropriate, I presume the reader would have it in prefererence to anything I could furnish myself:

REV. PATRICK O'BRIEN, LATE OF TENNESSEE, AND NOW THE PASTOR OF LAKE VIEW, CHICAGO.

The growth of the Church in Chicago keeps pace with the wonderfully increasing population, which now numbers some 750,000, and promises to double that number within the next quarter or half a century. Nearly half this great population is Catholic. There are two hundred and forty priests on duty in the Archdiocese, ministering in some two hundred churches and religious homes. New parishes are being rapidly organized and churches and schools constructed. Amongst the districts being organized is Lake View. The archbishop has around him faithful and zealous priests, ready, at his bidding, to labor for the good of souls and the welfare of the Church, in any manner he may suggest. Amongst them is the priest just appointed to organize the new parish at Lake View. We mention him because he has been identified with arduous missionary labor in Tennessee, from where, with a constitution shattered in the work of the ministry, he removed, two years ago, to Chicago, after having been adopted by the Most Rev. Archbishop. It was with reluctance that the bishop of Nashville consented to give Father O'Brien the necessary *exeat* to enable him to be affiliated with the Archdiocese of Chicago. The poor condition of his health made a change of climate necessary, and his Tennessee former congregations and numerous friends will be rejoiced to know that he is now fully recuperated, and that, after acting for the past two years as assistant priest in the Immaculate Conception Church of Chicago, he is appointed by the Archbishop to organize the new parish of Lake View In a few weeks the erection of the church will be commenced. In this the fine executive ability of Father O'Brien will be developed, and the Catholics of Lake View will find that the humble and unassuming pastor possesses abilities and stable qualities, whose merits will be increased with years. During the seven years of missionary career in this diocese, Father O'Brien endured severe hardships, not ordinarily connected with missionary labor. How admirably he bore himself amid most trying circumstances, will not soon be forgotten here. In 1878 he was in charge of the missions attached to Jackson, Tenn. On these missions every variety of missionary labor was represented, coupled with the hardships and privations familiar only to the pioneer missioners, who have traveled with their saddle-bags through the country. In the middle of August, 1878, he was allowed a vacation, which he did not enjoy. The cry of the Yellow Fever Plague brought him back to his scattered flocks, now increased by refugees from Memphis. There was scarcely a village in Tennessee, within one hundred miles of Memphis, but was, in a few short weeks, afflicted with the dreadful Yellow Fever Plague. While the eyes of the world were turned toward Memphis, in those days of harrowing memories, the terrible scenes and sufferings of many of the surrounding villages and country districts filled with refugees, were lost sight of The organized relief committees, and ample accommodations, surrounded with every luxury, dispelled, in a great manner, the terrors of the plague in Memphis. In life and death, everywhere their services were needed, the priests were together in ministering one to another in Memphis It was otherwise on the missions, where, unnoticed by the outside world, Father O'Brien's frail and delicate constitution was brought in contact with the worst features of the awful plague. The shot-gun quarantine was then the order of the day, and it was enforced even against the priest When all the Catholics, and others accepting his ministry, had been prepared for death at Grand Junction, Father O'Brien found himself quarantined, deprived of the necessaries of life, and confined in the houses in which he was ministering to the sick and dying. Having succeeded in boarding a passing train, he endeavored to get back to Jackson, but the train would not be allowed to stop there, and it had to dash through at the rate of thirty miles an hour, or its occupants accept the compliments of a shot-gun or rifle salute. For about twenty-four hours the good, devoted priest sought, in vain, somewhere to rest in Tennessee, and he at last found it in generous, hospitable and brave Clarksville, that did not close her gates against the refugees, and yet escaped the plague. He did not get much rest The cry came from Brownsville, and thither hurried Father O'Brien. There were about eighty Catholics residing in Brownsville and vicinity, and the number was increased by refugees from Memphis. The plague made desperate havoc among them, and the whole town was well decimated in a few weeks. During the time Father O'Brien remained ministering to the sick, and even helping to bury the dead, the hard floor of the little church—since blown down—being his bed at night. How he must have suffered during those terrible days and long, weary, dreamy nights, with the thought of dying without a priest to administer to himself the last sacraments, can well be imagined, especially by those who are in any way acquainted with the character, hopes and aspirations of a young priest, who, filled with religious zeal, has left home and kindred to become a soldier of the cross in foreign lands! God spared Father O'Brien for another, and even in some respects a greater trial. Three years later, whilst pastor at Jackson, a brother priest of the diocese, the late Rev. John F. Walsh, was stricken down with the small-pox. He had contracted it whilst ministering to a patient in Memphis, but unaware of that fact, was on a visit to Father O'Brien. When it became known that the case was one of small-pox, a rigid quarantine against the house was enforced Guards were placed at a convenient distance around it, and no one, not even the physician, was allowed to enter. The medical prescriptions and other necessaries were flung toward the front door, and picked up by Father O'Brien or the good old lady who was acting as his housekeeper. Thus confined, the devoted priest had to become physician, nurse, and everything else until his dear companion, to whom he was bound with fond affection as well as religious duty, breathed his last. One family especially—that of Captain McMullen, brother of the late Bishop McMullen—braved quarantine regulations and visited at the bed of the dying priest, as did also the Dominican Sisters. The undertaker sent a casket and screwdriver, which he never since claimed, and Father O'Brien had now to act as undertaker. Captain McMullen and Mr. Cunningham assisting in digging the grave, escaping to and from the cem-

4 *

etery amid the shades of night and the down-pouring rain torrents, the mad rigors of quarantine, which was to be continued for fourteen days after the death of Father Walsh During the years of his ministry in Jackson Father O'Brien did a great deal for the future of the Catholic Church. He completed the church, introduced Sisters, and established a school, and also purchased and paid for a cemetery. He was beloved by Catholic and Protestant alike. His quiet, calm, far-seeing methods and policy are the admiration of every one who came in contact with him. The Catholics of Lake View will find in him a PRIEST and a MAN who will be devoted to their wants and faithful in everything. His old friends in Tennessee regret that he has left them, but rejoice that his health is recruited, and congratulate him on his new appointment to the charge of Lake View, whose good people will, we hope, rally around him and enable him to erect, before many months, a church, a school, and a residence. *Ad multos anros!*

I now request the reader to accompany me while I describe the mode of attack, development, and destructive agency of this redoubtable plague.

## THE FEVER OF '73, AND WHERE IT WAS SUPPOSED TO HAVE GERMINATED.

The winter of the year 1873 began with a virulent outbreak of small-pox, while during the summer months, June and July, a malignant type of Asiatic cholera made its appearance. But the advent of these epidemics was only the prelude to the ravages the Yellow Fever was soon destined to make.

Although it appears a paradox, yet it is really true this plague, for the time, drives away, or rather becomes king of all other diseases. Victims of consumption and heart

## THE FEVER OF 'SEVENTY-THREE. 43

disease become perfectly yellow after death. I remember attending a man who fell off a house and who died soon after from the effects. His corpse would indicate he died of Yellow Fever. I believe were a man suddenly stabbed, his body would turn yellow after death during its prevalence.

The Fever Plague of '73 lasted during the months of September, October, and only ended about the 20th of November. During these three months, some sixteen hundred people, of whom at least one thousand were Catholics, fell victims. Almost every case that occurred during the first month proved fatal. The disease lasted generally from two to four days. The third was usually the dark or dreaded day. Making allowance for a moderate aperient, in all cases, the less medicine, the better hope for the patient. Patients who had the attention of five, and sometimes ten physicians, invariably died; while a plurality of those who had no medical aid, and who were often bereft the common comforts of life, survived. I remember an old Irishwoman by the name of Cody, residing in Second street, being stricken down with the Fever. She was the only soul in the large tenement where she lay. When I called she had not seen a living person, black or white, for some twenty-four hours. I had to draw her a bucket of fresh water every morning, before I went to a neighboring grocery for some lemons and crackers. The poor woman had to reach from her bed to an adjacent stove in order to cook what little she could eat. She lay sick in this manner for some two weeks, and, strange, this old lady recovered. Nursing, medicine and nutriment were to this poor woman negative luxuries. The world seemed to have left her no positive possessions, save old age, the Irish language, and a good conscience,—the latter a "salve" that proved more effectual than all the therapeutic theories of Wood or Smith. I believe it was Cicero who said, "*Animi cultus quasi quidam humanitatis cibus.*"

Sanguineous or corpulent persons, when attacked, had far less chances of recovery than cold-blooded invalids, infants, or old people. A vast majority of those who succumbed were the chief support (the bone and sinew) of their respective families. After the Fever, enfeebled, decrepit old men and shrivelled old women (to whom death would be a relief) might be seen sitting on their door-steps, or with drooping heads, wending their way to the church. You would almost be inclined to smile at the mockery of death taking the father or husband, and leaving a weak, thriftless widow with five, six and sometimes eight children to battle with the cold world; in other cases, the son, who might have been engineer or conductor on the railroad, or clerk in some respectable firm, giving, every Saturday evening, his week's wages to the support of his wife, aged father and mother, was almost sure to take the Fever and die, while they were left to starve, or worse than starve, outlive their fortunes. The poor people who ran away from the Fever were made still poorer, being obliged to support themselves for three months in a strange place, where they could earn nothing and had to buy everything; whilst those who took the disease at home, or were unable to get away, had to waste their hoarded savings for food, fuel, nurses, medicines, etc.

The nurses received from five to ten dollars a day, and some of these were of questionable repute. Several Irish families assured me they were robbed of everything during their sickness. Indeed, from the reckless behavior of some, it appeared providential that more depredations than were reported did not occur. Even the negroes did not care to expose their lives by nursing, while they could obtain provisions without hardship or danger. I recall the case of a negro who refused five and asked ten dollars to catch hold of a coffin handle with the undertaker and another man who had but one hand. The coffin contained the remains of a Miss Nolan, who died at her residence, corner of Alabama and Commerce streets.

Another pitiable instance of poverty and lack of friends occurred rear of John Hollywood's grocery on Hill street. It was a case where a husband had to leave his sick bed to help the undertaker to put his wife's coffin in the hearse. The poor man fell twice in his efforts to render assistance. This man was not a Catholic.

Where did the Fever of '73 first germinate? Some eight hundred yards from the steamboat landing was a wretched marsh, designated by the euphonic title of "Happy Hollow." With the exception of some three or four white families, it was mostly inhabited by a colony of negroes, whose reputation for cleanliness and sobriety was by no means enviable. A family of immigrants from Shreveport, La., (a city then infected with Fever) was said to have landed here, where they brought the Fever, and soon died. Whether the Fever did spread from this locality and cause, is at best but a surmise, which has never been satisfactorily solved. At all events, "Happy Hollow" did in '73, and does to this day, enjoy the reputation of being the garden spot, where the "spores" or "sporadic germs" flourished and spread throughout the principal parts of the city. Although decimated in 1878, there was not a single case of Fever amongst the negroes of Memphis in '73. Notwithstanding that about one-third of the population of Memphis belong to the colored race, still, to their credit, it must be said, they refrained from plunder and other depredations that would prove ruinous to so many, and could not be resisted by the then inefficient City authorities. A few threats were made, perhaps rather jocular than earnest, that the colored "Folk," being Fever-proof, would soon take possession of the city. In general, those people conducted themselves tolerably well, considering the many opportunities to the contrary that offered. For many persons the panic proved a great boon, having good wages, very little to do, and the best board, without any cost to them.

### CHURCHES AND EDUCATIONAL INSTITUTIONS OF MEMPHIS.

At the outbreak of Fever in '73, there were in Memphis four Catholic churches, viz.: St. Patrick's, of which Very Rev. M. Riordan was Pastor, and Fathers P. McNamara and A. Luiselli, assistants; St. Peter's (Dominican), the Pastor being Very Rev. J. A. Kelly, and Revs. Cary, O'Brien and Daly, assistants;

St. Bridget's, of which Rev. M. Walsh was Pastor, and Rev. D. A. Quinn, assistant; the Franciscan Monastery; Pastor, Lucius Buckholst; assistant, Father Aloysius Weiver. Each church had a parish school (averaging about 400 scholars each) attached.

Besides an orphan asylum (averaging 200 inmates), the Sisters of St. Dominic had charge of two select academies—St. Agnes and La Salette. Its spacious grounds, choice location and corps of excellent teachers contribute to render St. Agnes the leading institution of its kind in the Southern States. This seminary has sent out graduates to almost every State in the Union; while some of the first ladies of the South (Catholic and Protestant) revere St. Agnes as their beloved Alma Mater.

In addition to the two already mentioned, there was a third select academy for young ladies in Memphis at the commencement of the year '73. I refer to that excellent and exceedingly popular institution conducted by the Sisters of St. Joseph. As I shall have occasion to speak of this Sisterhood later on, I need only say that, should any of the Sisters who formed the "faculty" in '73 revisit Memphis, they would learn to their satisfaction that neither they, nor the good lessons they imparted, were forgotten by the children and young ladies of Memphis. Even to this day the mention of Mother Leone, and Sisters Immaculate, Antoinette, Irene, De Sales and Clarissa, I do not hesitate to say, would gladden the hearts and brighten the countenances of the young Misses whom they educated, edified and refined. I know it will revive fond memories in the hearts of their former pupils at St. Patrick's, when I assure them that their former teachers have not yet forgotten their little pupils, and still refer to Memphis as the "Dearest place on earth."

I beg leave, in proof of this assumption to insert the last three lines of a St. Joseph Sister's letter to me :

DECEMBER, 1886.
"I like Chicago, but, Oh ! not one fourth as well as dear old Memphis. The mere allusion steals a sorrow o'er me."

When we take into account that Chicago with her half million inhabitants almost frowns at the little shadow of Memphis, and that eight years have elapsed since those good Sisters left the city, the insertion is highly complimentary.

Catholicity in Memphis in '73, and to the present day, could also boast of another public institute for males. I refer to the Christian Brother College under the conduct and management of Brother Maurellian, a young religious of marked ability, who, with his courageous band of Brothers, did incalculable service to the Yellow Fever sufferers of '73, '78, and '79. At present, their college in Memphis is unquestionably the first institution for educational purposes between St. Louis and New Orleans—perhaps few in the country can equal it. As classical and practical teachers, the Christian Brothers are no longer second, but equal, if not superior to the Jesuits. At the Paris exhibition, and at all the great public exhibitions held throughout Europe and this country, the first prizes have been frequently awarded to the evident proofs of their skill and industry.

In mentioning the Pastors of Memphis, in '73, I unwittingly failed to name first of all the Bishop of the diocese, Right Rev. P. A. Feehan, now Archbishop of Chicago. To his mature judgment and prudent forethought, may be ascribed the edifying zeal and good order that distinguished his clergy during this trying ordeal.

## MOST REV. P. A. FEEHAN.

This distinguished Prelate was born near Thurles, Co. Tipperary, Ireland, Aug. 28, 1829. Having completed his theological course in Maynooth College, Co. Dublin, where he attained the highest honors of the institution, by direction of Most Rev. Peter Richard,

Archbishop of St. Louis, to which archdiocese he had been affiliated, was promoted to Sub-Deaconship while still in Maynooth. Soon after, he embarked for America, directing his course to St. Louis, where he was immediately ordained Priest, Nov. 7th, 1852.

After a pastorate of several years in one of the largest churches of St. Louis, he was appointed to the vacant See of Nashville, Nov. 1, 1865. He remained Bishop of Nashville fifteen years, when, Sept. 10, 1880, he was promoted to the Archiepiscopate of Chicago. At his departure from Nashville, there were in the diocese thirty churches, eleven religious, and fourteen secular Priests. At present his jurisdiction extends over 198 churches, 192 secular, and 78 Priests of religious Orders. In the city of Chicago there are more than sixty Catholic churches, and the Catholic population of the Archdiocese, is estimated at 450,000.

The following graphic synopsis of the Archbishop's life recently appeared in one of the Chicago daily papers:

"A Prelate of the greatest simplicity of character, Archbishop Feehan is one of the strongest minded men in the Catholic church of America. He never transacts his business in the newspapers; he never engages in rash controversy. Every priest in his charge has discovered the strength, the kindness, the staunchness, the justice and loyalty of the Archbishop They and their people know that he can neither be wheedled nor driven from the course his good sense and judgment elect on any question."

Although it may appear presumptuous of me to dilate on the qualities of one who is revered throughout Europe and America, still, as I have lived under his fatherly jurisdiction for more than nine years, I cannot in justice to my subject, overlook the ennobling virtues that adorn his life. His undisturbed patience, uncompromising firmness, and his sweetness and gentleness in commanding, have deservedly won for him the title of "Captain of the Memphis Martyrs."

The fearful calamities that threatened the very existence of his diocese, called into action the highest qualities of governor and spiritual guide. Circumstances placed life and death in his hands. Had he succumbed to the Fever, it is more than probable, (it may be regarded a moral certainty,) there would not be a Priest living to-day to relate the sad tale of Memphis' woes. It is a terrible responsibility to have to order any man to certain and speedy death. Even the stern judge falters in his speech, as he pronounces the last sentence of the law on a guilty culprit. If this good Bishop, instead of the warm, tender nature which God bestowed him, had a heart of adamant, he could not help being moved in this fateful discharge of duty. In his unflinching charity towards the Catholic laity of Memphis, he had to bury in his soul the sweetest names known to man—"friendship," "patriotism," "kinship," and "old school-companionship." It was Syrus who said, "*Amicum perdere est damnorum maximum.*" "To lose a friend is the greatest of all losses." In this narrow crisis of words I abjure the insinuation that the Bishop was cold or stern in sending his friends and countrymen to take charge of parishes which death seemed to take delight in vacating. The dignity of his position, and the absolute wants of his dying flock, precluded any display of sympathy. "*Servare cives, major est virtus patriæ patri.*" "To save the people is the greatest virtue in the Father of his country." If one, two, or a notable number of Catholics died in want of a Priest, the world would soon hear of it under the heading of "Cowardice"—a humiliating aspersion at any time, but a scandal in time of Fever.

I shall never forget that eventful morning when Archbishop P. A. Feehan came out on St. Bridget's altar (Memphis) to preach the funeral oration of twelve of his Priests who had just died during the Autumn of '78. Perhaps a similar event has not occurred within the last century in Europe or America. During the cholera that decimated Nashville, in '73, and all the plagues that visited Memphis, Archbishop Feehan never deserted his post. But knowing the heartfelt uneasiness any public reference to himself is sure to cause, I shall forbear to make further mention of his life for the present.

## CONDITION OF MEMPHIS AFTER THE FEVER OF '73.

As already stated, the number of those who died throughout the various parts of the city, during the Autumn months of '73, might be estimated about sixteen hundred. The Pastor of St. Bridget's Church, Rev. M. Walsh, had a "framed" list hung up in his church, giving the names of eight hundred of his parishioners who died in less than three months. Almost as many more, whose names could not be procured, also died in this parish. On the first Sunday after the Fever was pronounced no longer epidemic, the people who flocked to hear mass at St. Bridget's church presented a sorry spectacle. It was noticed the following morning in the daily papers, that there was not a man, woman or child in the church that was not dressed in mourning.

During the Autumn of this never-to-be-forgotten year, Memphis lost some of its best and most respected citizens. Besides some twenty nuns (amongst whom was the Mother Superioress of the Franciscan Convent), five Priests — Fathers O'Brien, Cary, Daily and

Sheehy, of the Order of St. Dominic, and Father Leo, a German, of the Franciscan Order,—fell victims. It appeared providential that no secular Priest of the diocese (although equally exposed) contracted or died of Fever this year.

### REV. D. O'BRIEN, O. P.
*(Died Oct 9, '73—Aged 42.)*

At the time of his last illness, Father O'Brien was Procurator of the Dominican Convent on Adam street. His priestly energy and unswerving zeal deservedly won for him the esteem and affection of the citizens of Memphis, both Catholic and Protestant. His innate talents and financial undertakings elicited the admiration of many of the leading business men of the city. Some time before his death, the "Order" concluded to demolish the old pastoral residence and erect a new convent in its stead. During its erection, Father O'Brien took particular delight at the progress of the new structure; and he anxiously awaited the day when he was to remove into it, and select a room in his new home. The good Priest's hopes were not to be realized. I distinctly remember the morning when he was first attacked with the Fever. As he entered La Salette Academy, he took a violent chill. With chattering teeth, he requested a brother Priest to hastily make note of some memoranda of deposits which he had not time to transfer to his ledger. He never left the bed on which he lay that morning. Had not God disposed otherwise, this clergyman, being full of life and energy, and in every sense a picture of prime health, might have done great things for his "Order."

### REV. B. V. CARY, O. P.

*(Died Oct. 7, '73—Aged 40.)*

Father Cary, another Priest, who, in addition to youth, health, and a gigantic frame, possessed talents that rendered his name conspicuous, not only in Memphis, but throughout the Southern States, became another victim to this dread plague. Returning from a sick call in Market street, he took the Fever on his way, and was never again seen on the streets.

### REV. J. R. DAILY, O. P.

Father Daily, the first and youngest Priest that died of Yellow Fever in Memphis, was of Irish-American parentage, and although in appearance a mere boy, yet he was a cautious and vigorous man in wisdom and intellect. He took the Fever in that part of Memphis known as "Happy Hollow," where, until his sickness, he spent the greater part of his days and nights, ministering to the sick.

This St. Stephen of the Memphis martyrs, died on the 27th of September, 1873, at the early age of twenty-seven years.

I am sorry to state a want of personal acquaintance deprives me giving in detail the life and charitable deeds of Father Leo, the Franciscan Priest, who was made a victim of the Fever in '73. He died on the 17th of October, and was then 45 years old. Indeed, the Fathers and Brothers of St. Mary's Monastery have not only aided and edified the sufferers, but have impersonated their great Founder, St. Francis, in all their deeds and virtues.

If the German Catholics of Memphis should ever become cold in the practice of their religion, and forget the good lessons they received in Fatherland, no part of this aspersion can be attached to the Priests of their nationality in Memphis. Those self-denying and Saintly Fathers have given, by their lives, quite a different lesson.

As I shall have at a later period, occasion to speak of the bravery and ennobling virtues of Father Sheehy, I shall spare the reader a repetition of his life. The five Priests that gave up their lives in '73, are now sleeping side by side in Calvary Cemetery. At the head of each is a small marble slab, giving the place of birth, age, and date of death.

To each of those Clergymen who died in the full vigor of youth and manhood we may aptly apply the words of Cicero: "*Nemo parum diu vixit, qui virtutis perfectæ perfecto functus est munere.*" "No one has lived a short life who has performed its duties with unblemished character."

Although the first severe frost had destroyed all traces of Yellow Fever in Memphis, still several months elapsed before the last of the refugees had returned to their homes. Consequently, the depression in government, mercantile, and labor bureaus was very discouraging. The pastors of the different churches had also serious cause to complain. Not only were they deprived of pew-rents and other church revenues while the Fever lasted, but for several months after, they had to bear up against this privation, as also, to aid those who returned, or remained destitute. The Priests and other Ministers living in Memphis at the time, have honestly earned the encomiums bestowed on them by their co-religionists throughout the States.

POLICE AND FIREMEN OF MEMPHIS.

While giving such favorable notice to the clergy whose mission is benevolence and charity, it would be an unpardonable oversight to ignore the bravery, perseverance, and heroic zeal of two municipal organizations—the Police-force and Firemen of Memphis. The former, under the leadership of Chief Athy, not only performed their civic duties to the satisfaction of the people, but, like ministering Angels, were often seen at the bedside of the poor and distressed. In several instances, those brave fellows brought food and clothing to the hungry and naked; and a blue-coated giant might often be seen bearing in his brawny arms the infant babe from its departed mother, on his way to the Sisters' Asylum. In the darkest hours of Memphis, it was a cheering sight to recognize the giant form of Phil. R. Athy, riding up and down the principal thoroughfares. His courtesy, genial smile, and manly salute will not soon be forgotten. For several years he was the terror of thieves, gamblers and idlers; while yet, in his social capacity, he was affable and gentle as a child. As he has been since called to his eternal reward, I do not hesitate to give utterance to my honest conviction, that his name deserves to be inscribed in golden letters among the galaxy of brave and true Memphis Irishmen. In Elmwood Cemetery there is many a huge marble shaft over the remains of distinguished sons of Memphis, but not one marks the ashes of a braver hero than Chief Athy.

The chief of the other department, another true son of Erin, has also been called to his final reckoning. Chief McFadden has won a place in the hearts of the Catholics of Memphis that shall not be effaced in this present generation. The chief and his "Boys," as they were sometimes called, were of the best bone and sinew of Memphis. Although they might be seen lazily lounging at the doors of their respective engine-houses, besides being ever on the alert to attend a conflagration, like a lion in his lair, each man was ready to spring forward to resent wrong, or relieve a sufferer. It was noticeable they most all had young and handsome wives and lovely children. It would cheer one's heart to see those smiling maidens and matrons standing on the stoop or porch, with heaving bosoms, waving words of encouragement to the "Boys" in oil-cloth, as they flew past their doors in the midst of fire and smoke. And many a modest Memphis Belle cast a loving side glance, as she recognized her affianced lover among the leaders of the van.

FRATERNAL AND BENEVOLENT SOCIETIES.

Like Northern and Eastern cities, Memphis, in -'73, and to the present day, has a moderate variety of benevolent and national societies. Of these, the "Order of Ancient

Hibernians," is the first and oldest Catholic Society. Two distinguished merchants of the city, Messrs. Gavin and Lilly, acted as president or vice-president of this body for several years. The next society in order of priority is that known by the chivalrous title: "Knights of Innisfail." Unlike the Hibernians, who allowed some very old men in their ranks, the Knights were all a chosen body of young, healthy, and, if I must say it, good looking men. I remember when they first appeared on the streets, in '73, decked in their new uniforms, they captured everything that could be captivated. Memphians, who heretofore had seen on their public promenades only men or boys wearing a few green or blue ribbons, were taken by storm when they saw a real military organization marching in measured step, signalled by fife and drum, with "plumed" hats and belted swords. When any of their members fell in death they accompanied his remains to the church in full regimentals. Over his casket, surounded by a mountain of flowers, were placed the regalia and sabre he wore in life. Like "warriors, they marched beside his remains" to the grave, and saw that he was buried as he lived, *a true "Knight."* Yet those athletic, well-shapen fellows were not really soldiers of war. I trust I will not excite any ill-natured feelings should I insinuate that in this Society a few of its members never sniffed the smoke of martial powder or heard an active cannon ball. The "Knights" had nobler ideas than those inspired by bloody war, which is a remnant of *barbarism*. Their chief aim was to aid the oppressed and distressed—and above all, to shield honor, and enhance the glory of maidens. That those young gents were favorites with the fair—and less-fair—sex. is evinced from the facts that all their Tournaments and Feasts were crowded with the young and the old of every nationality.

Other Societies, such as the "Clan-na-Gael," the "Literary," the "Catholic Knights," and the "Temperance Brothers," seemed to flourish and command a large membership. Of all the Catholic Societies of Memphis, I think none has appeared more conspicuous nor can boast of having done more lasting good for themselves and others than the "Temperance Societies" of Memphis. This Society was first organized in Memphis in 1872, by the Rev. D. A. Quinn, who was also elected President of the State Union. In '74 it claimed a membership of one hundred and fifty. After the removal of Rev. D. A. Quinn from St. Bridget's, the Society passed under the spiritual guidance of Rev. Wm. Walsh. This

Rev. gentleman, with his temperance recruits, during the Fever of '78, originated the Father Mathew Camp, which saved the lives of four hundred men, women, and children during the plague. The members of this society have done great charity in their time, and deserve all the encouragement a Catholic Priest or people can bestow. I recall with pleasure an occasion, in '73, when the bravery of the Memphis Temperance Societies and firemen was put to serious test.

A renegade Irishman died in Commerce street. He had a pew in the Episcopal Church. He sent for me as he was on the point of death. Having abjured his heresy, and seeing that he was truly penitent, I administered to him the last Sacraments. After his death, next day, his employer, a rich cotton merchant, called to see me to request that I would allow his remains to be interred in his (the merchant's) lot in Elmwood cemetery. With reluctance I consented. As he was about to leave, he remarked, by the way, that he had invited Dr. W——, the Episcopal minister to perform the funeral rites and preach the panegyric. I told him he should not do so. In angry tones, he replied, he would not have an "old Priest" around his departed friend. "The man had lost his senses," said he, "when you attended him, and I deny that he ever died a Catholic." Knowing this to be an utter falsehood, and seeing that the man had a child living who would inherit considerable property, I positively insisted on my refusal. He answered me by a very insulting remark, after which I thrust him down the front-door steps and recalled my first promise allowing his remains to be carried to Elmwood. Cursing me, he ran immediately for the Chief of Police office. I, also, dispatched an emissary to Chief of Police Athy. Both entered the office at the same time, and each demanded the protection of the police. The Chief, with a smile told my messenger he was very sorry he could not let me have the police, at the same time bowing to Mr. B—— he assured him he was very sorry he could do nothing in the matter. "The whole affair," said he, "is a church matter, wherein I am not authorized to interfere." This was all I wanted. When Mr. Ryan, then sexton of St. Bridget's church, returned, I immediately ordered him to notify the Temperance Society and the Firemen. It was about two hours after, when a brother of Mr. B—— returned with all manner of apologies. Knowing he had no police protection, and having learned in a very short time, that all the Irish Catholics were preparing for battle, he begged me as a "church man" not to foment a riot, and to overlook the insults of his brother, who, he said, when excited, was very reckless in his remarks. Seeing this man spoke as a gentleman, I told him there would be no trouble if he and his preachers kept away from the house of the deceased man. He was very willing to guarantee this, and departed thanking me sincerely. In less than half an hour after Mr. B—— had left the parsonage, there were some two hundred men, mostly Temperance and Firemen, surrounding the house where the corpse lay. A spokesman amongst them declared, that if old Doctor W—— came to preach over that Irishman, assuredly there would be one Episcopal minister less, and probably a number of corpses beside the one in question. As the minister did not appear, everything passed off quietly. Mr. B—— and his brother attended the funeral and sat on the church steps while the "Requiem" service was being read.

Whenever a Pastor or other Priest was in pecuniary need, he had only to apply to the firemen. These brave and obliging fellows would organize into various committees, go around and take the name and gift of every merchant within their respective precincts. Whenever they appeared at fairs, pic-nics, or other charitable devices, they were sure to make a grand success.

While extolling the virtues and ennobling qualities of the police force and firemen of Memphis, I trust I have not exhausted the reader's patience by such a protracted digression; but seeing that several of those men laid down their lives in the discharge of spontaneous acts of benevolence, while, altogether, they rendered incalculable service to the city and citizens, I consider it a duty to bestow "honor to whom honor is due."

### FATAL CONSEQUENCES OF THE FEVER.

With painful interest I now request the reader to follow me back to the subject of Fever.

The disease seemed to have taken a relentless grasp of the northern portion of the city, usually called "Pinch," where the Irish were the majority. Taking Market street for a base, or southern boundary, those streets that ran at right angles, Front, Main, Second and Third, were more than decimated. In a boarding-house, corner Front and Market, I attended twenty-one Fever cases. In this same street, the young and beautiful wife of Mr. G——, a rich cotton merchant, was taken from her helpless children. By some mistake, this lady was "prayed" for in the church on Sunday, and the undertaker went to take her measure for a coffin while she was yet living. A Mrs. T——, of this same street, after losing her husband, two daughters and a son, begged me to lend her money to fly with her two surviving boys "up North." Although wealthy, she could find no one willing to cash a thousand dollar check until I lent her the money. An accomplished young school-teacher, the pride of her family, Miss Nellie M——, with her uncle, died in this same street. Webb, O'Loughlin, Kelly, Daily, Madigan, and Shea were fatal names in Front street.

At the corner of Auction and Front, I remember having seen a most respectable lady (Mrs. Shea) and her two daughters stretched dead in the same room. Her youngest child, Lizzie, was dying in an adjoining room. Recognizing my voice, she begged me to give her a drink of water. The physician had forbidden her ice-water. Seeing there was no hope for the child's recovery, I considered it humane to gratify her longing. I filled a large bowl with cold water. The veins of her neck swelled out as she swallowed the cooling draught. Having sipped the last drop, with a smack of her lips, she bit off a large portion of the bowl and crunched it beneath her chattering teeth. Another young lady in

Second street crept out of bed at night and drank a full pitcher of water, after which she fell dead. In this street, corner Jackson, I and another Priest called to see a family named L——. The entire household were down with the Fever. While I was giving the last Sacraments to the wife and husband in the same bed, the other Priest, a few feet distant, was hearing the confession of the son, then about twenty-one years old. I invited this young clergyman to see some three other families. The last, consisting of a mother and two daughters, in a dying condition, seemed to satisfy his zeal for that day. He begged to go home on "pressing" business. This family all died except a little boy, then about six years old. The father, who had considerable wealth, appointed his employer, a Mr. W——, Administrator. This man gave charge of the boy to a Mrs. N——, a *bigoted* Protestant. Hearing of his whereabouts, I induced the boy's uncle to secrete him from his guardian. He did so. A month after, I met the Administrator. Unbuttoning his overcoat, he produced a legal document. "Here, Mr. Quinn," said he, "I have an order from the court for this young man's and your arrest for kidnapping my ward." If this order was genuine, he failed to execute it,—perhaps more for his own sake than for any grace he wished to extend to me. The child, however, was brought back again, after Mr. W—— had promised to send him to the Christian Brothers' College in a year or two from date. At present, I have been informed the boy, or rather young man, has entirely ignored the faith of his fathers. Several such cases of proselytism, having occurred in this way, should be a warning to Catholics never to allow non-Catholics to have charge of their property or children.

The following instance is even more deplorable, from the fact that the children to whom I refer are to be deprived—perhaps for life— of the advantages of civil and religious education. Two girls, children of an Irishman who died in '73, were by some means given to an American family living in the woods, some four miles back of Covington, Tennessee. In company with a lady from Mason-depot, who acquainted me of their whereabouts, I went out to see if there was any prospect of having those children brought back and given to the Sisters or some Catholic families of Memphis. After frequent inquiries as to where this man lived in the wilderness, we at last reached his place of residence. The dwelling was a wretched log hut, near which stood an old, dilapidated barn. There we recognized the children.

From our first arrival, the unkempt farmer viewed us with sinister suspicion. As the children, who appeared to be sadly neglected, approached, we acquainted the gentleman as to the object of our Sunday visit. I call him gentleman more through constraint than courtesy, for although he was the only living specimen of his sex residing in the locality, his conduct towards me and the lady with me forfeited every claim to good breeding or hospitality. As he compressed a quid of tobacco between his blackened teeth, he drawled out an asseveration, to which he prefixed and affixed the Adorable Name, that any son of an Irishman that would try to take those children would first receive the contents of a murderous shot-gun, to which he made an incoherent, but very suspicious motion. Not feeling particularly desirous to carry home with me a full charge of country buckshot, I considered it prudent to decamp, not, however, before I expressed my sincere regret that the children should be thus exiled with a savage in a savage wilderness.

Another little girl, named Mollie Taft (at present adopted by a respectable gentleman, Owen L——), was taken to a county village on the Paducah railroad by an itinerant Preacher, and given to a Protestant family. I wrote for the child, but only received impertinent and defiant answers. I consulted a friend, who was a city detective. He told me the only thing I could do was to have the court appoint me Guardian. Then I could demand and re-take the child. I intended to follow this advice, in case "all fruit failed." From recent experience of court-house etiquette, however, I had no desire to have myself appointed legal Guardian, so I expected to accomplish my object by an endeavor to scare or "bluff" the Preacher. I had plausible and some very knotty facts on my side. Writing to the Minister, I stated that I had several witnesses who were prepared to vouch in court, that on a certain Sabbath evening he wheedled into his buggy an Irish girl, twelve years old, and drove with her into the woods, in the direction of Overton station, and that, ever since, no satisfactory account of her whereabouts had been given. Such proceedings on the part of a Minister having no control of her person or religion, but heretofore an entire stranger, I contended, in the eyes of the law, would appear very like a case of "kidnapping," which charge I would prefer, unless the child was returned herewith. My warning had the desired effect. Seeing that his action appeared very suspicious, the Preacher went immediately to the parties to whom he gave the young girl and begged them to return her at once, or else he would be a "ruined" man. After a lapse of three or four days, the girl was brought back to the church by a rural escort, who spoke as though it was a part of his errand, not only to return the child "safe and sound," but also to exhibit a very vile specimen of slang profanity.

Lest there should be any doubt as to the correctness of this narration, I simply give the initials of the Preacher's name, V——, and the parties who wished to adopt the child, H——. A staunch and good-natured Irish miller (James Mehan), still living in Kerrville, Tenn., can give a graphic account of this episode.

But Priests, during the Fever, had more deplorable and difficult cases that demanded their attention. In some instances, children whose parents had died, or friends left the city, were taken into houses of doubtful repute. One example will answer for three or four of the kind that came under my notice during the Fever of '73.

A young girl, about sixteen years of age, named Jennie ——, a convert from Protestantism, and about eighteen months from Ireland, was induced by parties whom she considered very nice young ladies, to go to their residence and remain there until her married sister would return from the North. The poor girl, having no sinister suspicions, being glad to find what, so far, was very hard to find, a good home, willingly accepted their offer. After the Fever, a companion, and christian namesake, told me of Jennie's whereabouts. I consulted Chief of Police Athy, who directed officer M—— to accompany me to the place. Having entered the house, the Officer rapped with his baton, when to our surprise and satisfaction Jennie herself was the first to appear. She seemed anxious and glad to leave. As the young woman had some costly clothing we concluded it was best to have her trunk and all leave at the same time. Accordingly, Jennie was called to give an inventory of her wearables. Her Prayer-book and Beads were amongst the first articles recovered. In the hurry of the moment, some of the young woman's garments were either purposely withheld or could not be found. This was no source of trouble to big Officer M——. He asked Jennie to show him anything that "looked" like her property, when with the least indication of her head or hand, he stowed into her trunk not only what she readily recognized, but everything that bore a doubtful resemblance to it. The only satisfaction he afforded the misguided inmates who protested, was the threat, that the whole place would be "pulled" or burnt in less than a month. The Catholic Orphanage, which is in the vicinage of this wretched "den" was the scene of great disturbance for several nights after Jennie had left. Many shots were fired in the direction, and murderous threats were made by ingratiated male friends of the young lady, suspecting that she was yet concealed in the Orphan Asylum. The young lady was sent to a good Shepherd convent, where she has ever since remained a pious and most exemplary Magdalen.

Some days after this event, I met the Irish giant policeman on the street. After showing me a letter he received, with a pair of Scapulars from Ireland, I reverted to our late encounter. "M——," said I, "I think some of those things we took that day did not belong to the child." "Oh, Father," said he, "don't mind that—sure they don't need anything out there; I wish the whole place was burnt, Father, if it were only for the sake of the Orphans." While I could unite in the same wish, I still thought his notions of equity were rather primitive.

This good man lost his only daughter Maggie in '73. She was a modest and beautiful young lady of some seventeen summers. I say "summers," for she had no winters with this kind and good-natured father, who loved her as the apple of his eye. You may talk with him for an hour, yet he would always wind up his discourse with tear-fraught eyes, and the almost whispered name of his poor " Maggie." While visiting a patient, a little black-and-tan dog that belonged to a negro happened to bite me. Officer M—— heard of it. A week after, I met him. "Father," said he, "I fixed that brute." "What brute?" "Oh, the dog that bit you, Father." "Did you kill him?" "Yes, Father. Between ourselves, I could get into trouble, for I had no warrant. But I scared the 'darkies,' by threatening to have them all brought to court, when they begged me to kill the dog and go no further."

Amongst the homeless waifs of '73 was a beautiful little child named Katie T——. Her dying mother left her in my charge, begging me to get her a nice home after the Fever. I promised to do so, and took the child (three years old) in my arms to the church, after the mother had impressed her last farewell kiss on its velvet cheeks. I had given this child for adoption to some seven different respectable families, who all, after a few weeks or months, returned her on account of her persistent aversion to men. It would appear that no wheedling could induce little Katie to shake hands or kiss him who offered to be a father to her. Whether this was sufficient cause to reject or recommend, I forbear to state ; at all events it was the alleged reason for sending the poor child away from many a comfortable home. But although Mis-Fortune and Miss Kate seemed to be inseparable companions, still it would seem old dame, or Mrs. Fortune, had an eye to the child all the time. A lady in Hongkong, a Mrs. C——, had made frequent but unsatisfactory inquiries after the child and its mother. Hearing the mother had died of Fever, she wrote me offering to educate Katie until she would be a grown young lady. It seemed this Mrs. C—— was once a ward of Katie's mother, who taught her the millinery trade. Having met an English tea merchant in San Francisco, she married and went with him to China. Mrs. C——, in her first letter, sent me a check for twelve hundred dollars, directing me to buy a certain homestead for the child. Besides several chests of most costly clothing and a box of jewelry, valued at fifteen hundred dollars, this good lady continued to send, on an average, some two or three hundred dollars a year to Katie and her grandmother. She was educated by the Sisters of St. Agnes Academy, Memphis. At present, I learn she is a most beautiful and accomplished young lady and an ornament in the "circle" wherein she moves.

Mr. John L——, a wealthy and respected wine-merchant of Memphis, adopted another Yellow Fever waif in '73. The child's parents died of the Fever. As this gentleman has no children of his own, little Mollie will likely be a rich young lady at some future day. At present, she is an adept in music, painting and literature, towards the cultivation of which, her adopted mother has spared neither pains nor expense.

The strangest, and in some instances the most unaccountable features of human nature were developed during the prevalence of the Fever. Side by side, you would see undaunted heroism and vile cowardice; miserly penury and open-hearted philanthrophy. Ladies and gentlemen occupying high positions in life might be seen going from house to house aiding the poor and suffering, while others either kept aloof or offered their services at the highest price. A dying wife assured me her husband ran away and left her and two children in a dying condition. In some instances a child would be afraid to visit his parents, and a brother refuse to visit a sister or brother. In these cases human sympathy was exposed to an awful strain; and considering the probable, if not always fatal danger of visiting a sick person, it was hard to blame them for not risking their lives. Hence, if it were not for the Priests and Sisters, hundreds would have died without a living soul to administer to their extreme wants or have their bodies prepared for decent burial. I remember two instances which were especially sad. One was a case where the Fever-stricken wife had lain from three o'clock, P. M., until midnight beside her dead husband. The parties resided in Commerce street. Feeling it unnatural to let the woman remain all night with a corpse, I went round for more than two hours, trying to induce some one to remain with this poor widow. At last, when it was about 12 o'clock, midnight, a Fireman volunteered to keep watch. As this woman had no money, it might be expected that she would have few or no friends.

But the other instance I am going to relate refers to parties who were wealthy, and who, before the Fever, had hosts of friends. One morning, as I entered their house on Main street, I saw Mrs. M. B—— stretched dead beside her little pet-daughter, Mollie, who was also on the point of death. There was not a soul around to look after the corpse. I had to walk several blocks before I could find any one who had courage enough to enter the residence. The next morning I re-visited the house. Little Mollie again called me to her bedside. Although she was in ill condition to weep, her little eyes were moist with tears. "Oh, Father," said she, "I do not like to die and leave papa alone." I expressed the hope that God might let her live for her papa's sake, when she corrected me: "I must die, Father," said she; "mamma appeared to me last night at the window, and told me I should go with her." These words, whether the ravings of a fevered brain or an intuitive perception of her approaching end, struck me very forcibly. At all events, it was only a question of a few hours when she obeyed the real or imaginary call of her mother. That same evening, as I happened to be passing along Main street, I re-entered the house as far as the chamber door. As I gazed on the two lifeless forms, mother and child, rigid and dishevelled, after their hard struggle with death, I felt as though relieved, seeing that the dread battle was over and won, for on either countenance there glowed a placid smile. Although thirteen years have elapsed since that innocent child rendered her soul to its Maker, I distinctly remember how serious and awe-stricken she appeared before death. I had to visit her three times before she felt prepared to bid me a final farewell. Her last words sank deeply into my soul: "Oh!

Father, it is a hard thing to die and appear before God." Would that those who have committed more sins in one hour than this child, were she to live a hundred years, would take a lesson from her last words.

> "How shocking must thy summons be, O ! death,
> To him that is at ease in his possessions ;
> Who, counting on long years of pleasure here,
> Is quite unfurnished for that world to come."

The instance of a young lady who died in Market street affords a touching, as well as an edifying example. In response to a sick call, Father Cary, a Dominican Priest, called at the residence of this young lady. After hearing her confession and administering Extreme-Unction, he promised to return with the Holy Viaticum the following morning. The good Priest was unable to keep his engagement, for he took the Fever from this house and was dead himself before the girl whom he had so recently prepared.

It must be remembered that messengers dispatched to the Priest's residence, to notify him of urgent calls, were very often disappointed. The Priest was obliged to spend the greater part—in fact, most of his time—away from home, attending those who had anticipated his departure in the morning. In such cases, the parties had either to await the Priest's return, or indite the names and addresses of those to be attended, on a slate placed for the purpose at the door of the pastoral residence. This arrangement was expedite, for the reason that it afforded the visiting clergyman a selection of those streets that had the most "calls," which, if visited promiscuously, would be impossible to attend.

As I was passing along Front street, at the intersection of Market, the young lady's uncle came up and begged me to call and see his niece. Although the house was within the limits of St. Peter's parish, I thought in charity I would comply. As I entered, the mother whispered to me that Father Cary could not give her the Sacrament, as she was continually retching. Overhearing these words, the patient sat upright in the bed and said, "Father, for the love of Jesus Christ, give me the Holy Sacrament before I die. If you do, I will pray for you while I will be in Heaven. I will not throw it up, Father." Considering it impious to refuse under these circumstances, I gave her the Holy Viaticum. To the astonishment of those looking on, and my own amazement, after raising her eyes towards Heaven, and then gently closing them, she fell back on the pillow a corpse. There are several ladies still living in Memphis who have been witnesses of this fact. A few days after, the young lady's uncle took the Fever. He had joined the Freemasons, and had lost the faith. His sister sent for me. After hearing his confession, and receiving his Masonic pin and badge, I anointed and gave him the "last blessing." As I took his hand to bid him farewell, with an anxious look he said, "Won't you give me what you gave Celia?" The poor fellow had not made his First Communion. I remonstrated, but to no purpose. "Father," said he, in a pitiful tone, "don't let me die without it." On the promise of a pious young lady, to instruct him as best she could, I gave him the Holy Sacrament. After attending a few other sick people, I called again that same evening. He was dead. In the next house, I could hear the pitiful wailing of a bereaved wife, whose husband, of the fire department, had just expired.

Lovers and devotees of romance will find the two following cases especially interesting:

A wealthy and respectable young widow (a Mrs. H——) residing in North Memphis, besides two promising and intelligent boys, was also blessed in the possession of two favored daughters, called Lizzie and Mamie. As the latter is still living, and on the high road to happiness and conjugal prosperity, my remarks shall be confined to the short life and saintly death of Lizzie. Having reached the golden age of virgin maturity, besides possessing all the fascinations that beauty, wealth, and refined culture could afford, this maiden plighted her betrothment to a young city merchant (a brother of one of the prominent clergymen of the city). In the prime of manhood, his pleasing address and athletic physique afforded him welcome access to the society of ladies and gentlemen, who, if they did not feel disposed to admire his handsome face, could not fail to appreciate his wit and manly demeanor. The mother and daughter fairly idolized this young man and his saintly brother. It would seem as though Heaven had destined Lizzie and Joe an inseparable twain. Before the epidemic, Joe spent most of his spare time at the home of his future fair young bride. But it was only when his enamored "fiancée" was prostrated with Fever that he manifested his devotion and constancy. All his days and nights he spent at her bedside, anxiously awaiting the dreadful crisis. Some ten physicians were called for consultation. All that money and medical skill could accomplish were put to the utmost test; but in vain. Even the merits of Prayer and Sacrifice did not move that God that "spared not the life of His only Son." Old grim death stepped in between this loving couple, and wrenched asunder the clasped hands and the hearts they would unite in wedlock. In the death of this young lady, the mother felt wrung out of her very soul the almost adored image of her affections; while the young man's hopes were blighted and his feelings blunted, if not entirely indurated.

Some time after, as I was on a visit to my native country, I saw this young man's brother making the Jubilee in the little chapel of Bourna, near Roscrea. My brother, Rev. Peter Quinn, then a Priest of that district, pointed him out to me as we were viewing the church. I motioned him to follow me out in the chapel yard. When I informed him who I was, and that I resided in the same house with his brother for seven years, his swimming eyes could no longer conceal their heavy burden. There was a marked resemblance between himself and his departed brother. With yearning anxiety he importuned me to let him know how Father Martin died; what became of his money and his valuable gold watch and chain. I sadly informed him his brother died penniless; that even the vestments that were encoffined with his remains were donated by the hand of charity, and that I had seen myself his brother's last dying scroll, "willing" his watch and chain to a faithful friend who never forsook him in health, sickness, or death. I told him, also, all I could remember about his first cousin, Father Michael Meagher's death.

Thinking the poor fellow had now exhausted his store of interrogatories, I reached for his hand to take leave, when another cloud of anxiety overspread his pale countenance, as he begged of me to tell him where his brother Joe was. In this, I was completely non-plussed. I could only say that his brother had left the city some three years previous, and that it was probable he had not heard of Father Martin's death. Although this honest fellow seemed quite indisposed to any form of consolation, he seemed to brighten up when I expressed the hope that Joe, like the prodigal son, might one day surprise his friends and return to his father's house.

The foregoing romance recalls to us the beautiful lines of Moore:

"Life is a waste of wearisome hours,
 Which seldom the rose of enjoyment adorns,
 And the heart that is soonest awake to the flowers,
 Is always the first to be touched by the thorns."

The other case, savoring of romance, was this: I was called to attend a young and recently married couple,—both sick in the same bed. They lived in Front street. As it would be certain and speedy death to remove either one, I was in a quandary as to how I should hear their confessions. The wife, noticing my embarrassment, said, in a half-suppressed smile, "I guess I did nothing John cares about." I saw this couple next morning, both dead. Veritable! Their hands were locked! As I gazed upon the manly brow of this brawny knight, and the delicately-moulded features of his fair companion, I felt as though death had made a pitiless stroke. Recalling her last words of the previous evening, "I guess I did nothing John cares about," I could wish that all wives had such a clear conscience in their last moments, and that every married couple might be united like them, hand in hand, in life and death.

### WALTHAL INFIRMARY.

This building, improvised for a Yellow Fever hospital, stood on Promenade street, near Market, facing the Mississippi river. It was a large and commodious building. Here, several poor persons, and others who could not afford medical attendance, were brought for treatment. Rooms were portioned off for men and women. The Priest was expected to visit this hospital every day. In every instance where he failed to make a spontaneous, he was required to make a compulsory visit. The medical treatment, the nurses, and general attention, I am pleased to say, were satisfactory. To a young clergyman, however, (as I was at the time) it appeared rather uncomfortable to see so many invalids congregated.

Heretofore, the Priest had only to visit the sick, more or less isolated, in their respective residences. But here was mortifying humanity by the wholesale. The nurse (generally a non-Catholic) had no idea of what was necessary for the decent administration of the last Sacraments. The Priest had to bring everything himself. Clergymen who attend hospitals, penitentiaries, etc., readily understand these difficulties. However, in those instances, the Priest had generally the right to order the inmates of the room to absent themselves while he was hearing a patient's confession. This was not feasible in Walthal Infirmary. The patients, being all bed-ridden, and of different creeds, were either unwilling, or unable to leave. The only resort for the attending clergyman was to draw as near as possible, and be ready to catch the least whisper of the penitent, who, if somewhat deaf (as was frequently the case), made the effort very distressing. As the Priest sat beside the patient, it was dreadful to hear the stertorous breathing of those giving up the ghost in different parts of the room. In the corridors, one was sure to see three or four corpses every morning.

While hearing a poor man's confession in a ward in which there must have been twelve or fifteen others, endeavoring to live or die, I noticed before me a man who had just drawn his last breath. Two strong colored nurses stood over him immediately. Turning the sheet on which he lay over his body, they lifted and carried the still warm "remains" out in the corridor. There stood a long deal box. In this they deposited the corpse. The box was immediately covered, and securely nailed, taken down stairs and into the street, where a horse and wagon were awaiting, not this body alone, but a full load of human flesh.

Lest the foregoing remarks should hurt the feelings of any one still living, who had been engaged in Walthal Infirmary, I beg to state that, under the circumstances, much better could not be done. The adage says, "*Constans aut lenis, ut res expostulet esto.*" "Be firm or mild, as the occasion may require."

INCIDENTS OF THE FEVER OF 1873.

In some particular instances, the patients died before they had sufficient strength to swallow the Viaticum; while others, having "received," were obliged to vomit. These cases were very embarrassing, because the Priest had to collect the half dissolved particles from the lifeless tongue or basin in which they were deposited, and put them into a separate Pix, to prevent infection. Some Priests consumed these particles during Mass the following morning.

Ghastly strange and some very ludicrous things occurred during this eventful time. A young Priest told me he was badly scared one day in a house on Commerce street, between Second and Main streets. Being summoned to attend a sick person, he went right to the bed where he thought the patient lay, seized the man by the hand, shook his head, and told him to make his confession. There was no move. He shook him again, when, to his horror, he saw it was a corpse, which he mistook for a sick man in the next room.

I remember seeing Father Walsh, who died in '78, enter the pastoral dining room, his face and shirt-bosom bespattered with black vomit. The Doctors prescribed a little bag of assafœtida for all the Priests to wear in their bosoms during the prevalence of the Fever. One day, as a number of Priests were recreating themselves after dinner, at St. Bridget's parsonage (in '73), a young Priest stood up, and with animation said: "Gentlemen, I have borne this horrid thing long enough," whereupon he released his neck from string and bag, both which he flung into the fire, saying, "Here, let me die if I will, but I shall never be brought to my grave with such a detestable odor." Indeed, next to capital punishment or exile, the compulsory wearing a bag of assafœtida for three days is the most ignominious punishment to which a man of good odor can be consigned. Except Sin alone, it compounds all the fetidness decaying nature can furnish.

Although the Negroes escaped the Fever of '73, still they were panic-stricken, and mortally afraid whenever any strange event or sickness occurred amongst themselves. One early morning of the month of October, '73, near the corners of Main and Jackson streets, a group of half terrified Negroes surrounded the carcass of a mule that lay stretched in the middle of the street. While the men shook their heads in ominous silence, the women exhausted all the portentous ejaculations of Negro verbiage. At last, a Negro whose cropped, but frosted hair bespoke the winter of "three score and ten," in the capacity of spokesman, said: "Colored sisters and brothers: when de Feber takes de mule, de Nigger ha n't got no show." This process of reasoning, although contrary to Christian cosmogany, did not militate against the theories of Darwin, who acknowledged no distinction between animal protoplasms. In fact, the colored spokesman, according to the latter writer, made a logical deduction, predicting no escape for his people when evidence showed the "grade" above and below his race were attacked by the Fever.

The following, although occurring some two weeks before the Fever of '73 appeared in Memphis, is such a thrilling narrative that I cannot discard it. And, as there is no question of honor or honesty at stake, I will locate where the incident occurred, in the residence of a kind and most charitable lady, living near the intersection of Third and Market streets. I have previously stated, a virulent outbreak of Cholera preceded the Yellow Fever of '73. The good landlady of this residence took a violent case of Cholera. Although cramps, at intervals of five and six minutes, threatened to make short work of her life, still, owing to medical skill and frequent rubbing and mustard bathing, she soon became convalescent. During severe shocks, her reason occasionally became unsettled. The physician left a small bottle to allay the spasms, prescribing a teaspoonful to be given every three hours. By some unfortunate mistake, a little white bottle which the Lady herself had secreted behind a clock on the mantel, was produced, and mistaken for the bottle given by the Doctor. When the patient saw the nurse pouring some of its contents on a teaspoon, she screamed and remonstrated with all her might. The neighbors in the vicinage hearing the unnatural shrieks, ran immediately to the house, rushing into the room without ceremony. All concluded the woman had again lost her senses. A man, and some three women, held the patient down with efforts that required all their reserved strength. Every attempt to give the medicine was unavailable. In the meantime the Priest was despatched for. He being an old friend of the sick Lady, it was hoped, would calm her fears and restore reason. No sooner had the patient seen the Priest than she again screamed "Poison! Murder! Mercy!" The Priest was sorry to see his friend in such a phrensy. He addressed her gently, and did all he could to calm her feelings. But the patient only became the more disconsolate. Seeing this, he concluded like the other bystanders, that the Doctor's medicine was the only thing that would quiet her nerves. Accordingly, he assisted by holding the patient's hands, while the nurse poured out a teaspoonful. By a superhuman effort the woman wrenched her hands loose, and grasping the bottle from the nurse's hand dashed it in pieces against the marble mantel. After this struggle she became perfectly quiet.

The Priest seeing there was no immediate danger, returned to the parsonage. Not wishing to go back again, being somewhat "*piqued*" at the bipartition of his magnificent gold chain which the patient in her struggles wrenched asunder, he requested me to visit the sick woman before night, fearing she might take a relapse and die without the Sacraments. I obeyed his orders. As I entered the sick room, I was surprised to hear the patient greet me with a very pleasant salute. She appeared perfectly calm and collected, although faint and exhausted. Addressing me by name she said : " Father, the terrors of death are yet in my heart." Imagining she referred to her attack of Cholera, I allowed she ought to be very thankful for such a narrow escape. "It is not that, Father; don't you know the neighbors, and even the Priest, wanted to *poison* me?" I began to have misgivings that her "ravings" might lead to another attack, when she soon composed my fears, or rather startled me by the appalling fact itself. "The dose which they would have me take was from a bottle of strychnine, which I concealed behind the clock before I took sick ; when I saw it in the nurse's hand I roared Poison! and Murder! All the horrors of death came before me, until I snatched the bottle and broke it. I beg you to excuse me to Father ——— for being so rude, and I am so sorry to break his chain."

After hearing this frightful tale, and all but miraculous escape, I assured the good Lady her refusal to take a dose of strychnine was entirely orthodox ; and that if general etiquette required her passive compliance, the present instance was carrying domestic politeness a little too far. I had to join in the laughter she excited when, as I left the sick room, she said: "The bottle did me one service—it cured me of the Cholera." When I returned and informed the Priest of his appalling mistake he refused to believe the woman had her right mind, and he was taken to his grave without being convinced.

I have already mentioned, that besides the important, if not imperative duties of administering the last Sacraments and Rites of the Church, taking care of homeless waifs, and aiding the sick and suffering, another serious duty devolved on the Priest during the horrors of Fever. It was the taking charge of money, jewels, deeds, &c., of those who had no trusty friends around them at the moment of death. If prudence discouraged, at least Christian Charity, forbade the Priest to ignore this important duty. I cannot refrain from relating an instance of this kind.

A widow in rather comfortable circumstances died in Jackson street (Mrs. M——). She was a favorite amongst the Catholics, and had merited the blessing of every poor Irish family in the neighborhood. She took the Fever. The morning she expired, I happened to call at her house, and found the room in which she lay filled with people. It would seem as though, in spite of all the terrors of Fever, the neighbors, "white" and "colored," wanted to see Mrs. M—— before she died. I had given her the last Sacraments the day before, and had just concluded the blessing "In articulo mortis," when an old woman whispered to me that all her money, jewelry, and valuables were locked up in the bureau drawer. I quietly approached the dying woman, and asked her for the keys. To my surprise, she was speechless. In this emergency I scarcely knew what to do. The lady's oldest daughter was at the convent at Joliet, Ill., and the younger one was but a child. In the absence of any responsible party, I feared to leave her valuables among such a promiscuous crowd. Having nothing better, I took a poker and pried the drawer open. While engaged, I glanced over at the dying woman. To my astonishment, her face was lit up with a smile. It was well I opened the drawer, for it contained, besides her gold watch, chain, and jewelry, some valuable papers, and a few hundred dollars in greenbacks. Her two daughters, Joe and Minnie, are now accomplished young ladies, and no doubt appreciate these souvenirs of a mother's memory. When the Fever had subsided, I remember having, "for safe keeping," ten silver, and five gold watches, besides several lockets, chains, bracelets, and rings. Some cherished heirs or dear friends of the departed are now wearing those fond tokens of brighter days.

Before I proceed further in my narration of personal reminiscences, I wish to state that in all the examples I have made bold to relate, it has been far beneath any motive of mine to mention any fact solely for the sake of gaining the popular ear, when the same might wound the feelings of the parties concerned, or their friends. Although I have witnessed many sad cases of perfidy, intemperance, tyranny, and cowardice, I have studiously overlooked them, with the hope that the Father of Mercies will do the same. In all my references, I wish it to be distinctly understood that, as the glory of God is the primary object of this little work, I single out examples that I believe to be most edifying; and that, wherever I specify names or streets, I simply wish to recall in *fond recollection* to the living, the ennobling virtues of the "departed" whom they knew and loved.

This protracted, but I trust judicious explanation, has almost caused me to lose sight of the little incident I was going to relate.

About half past four, one fine morning in September, '73, a messenger rang the night bell of the pastoral residence. After a moment's enquiry I learned it was a sick call. Making all possible haste, I accompanied the little girl to the house where the patient resided. It belonged to an American Protestant family who had run away from the Fever and left Miss B——, a domestic, and her little sister in charge. Seeing the little girl who called me to visit her sister had the Fever, also, I ordered her into an adjoining room, where I heard her confession. In a few moments she lay beside her sister. After anointing the two, I endeavored to procure them whatever nourishment they might need until I could get a nurse, and promised to revisit on the morrow. On calling next day, I found the little girl dying—the other beyond all hopes of recovery. The elder sister told me in a faint voice she had some little "things" to dispose of. As I feared I could not remember everything, I took a sheet of note paper on which I pencilled down the jottings of her last "Testament." After she had "willed" the few dollars she had saved,— part for Masses, and part for her mother in

Ireland,—she directed me to give her chain and locket to Nellie C——; and sliding a gold ring off her finger, "Father," said she, "give this to Mary M——; tell her to wear it, and pray for me." Her Prayer-book was to be placed near her head, and her Beads in her hands, before she was to be encoffined.

A strange feeling crept over me as I noted these trifles. It was the poorest "will" I ever indited—and yet, I felt it all the more sacred to execute. Unlike the stocks and deeds of the wealthy, that only forestall so many impossible, if not sinful obligations, this young maiden's inventory revealed a heart full of Faith, Friendship and Love. Before she felt herself worthy to face God, she wished to divest herself of the few baubles poverty had thrown in her way; and taking only the two emblems of her religion, she felt as though she was fully equipped for the journey of eternity.

Were we permitted to cast a glimpse over the Angel's great record of "Good and Evil," I doubt not but this girl carried from her humble pallet a greater wealth of sterling virtues than those mighty aristocrats who, when dying, were mirrored in plated glass and surrounded by artificial firmaments of blazing lights and golden tapestry. This young female was but a type of her class. The truest, the purest, the most faithful specimens of womanhood that ever crossed from the shores of Europe, are the Irish servant girls of America. Women in the various other walks of life have their "ups" and "downs"; while some lose courage and fall, others, spurning the smiles and frowns of fortune, remain true and faithful; but the Irish servant girls have always been a class of staunch Catholics. For an honest penny, any one of them will stoop to clean the marble steps of her master's door, but not for all the gold and bonds in his safe would she allow him to take her hand or kiss her cheek. These girls are the militant vanguard of the christian army. Although continually exposed to the votaries of Lust, Intemperance, and Atheism, yet they remain as pure as God made them. Let fashionable maidens and opulent matrons—yes, let even the toilsome housewife hold back. Their exposure, temptations and privations, are inconsiderate when we come to think what these faithful servants have to see, hear and suffer. Honor, then, to those Handmaids who fast while others feast, and who worship and pray in the midst of Paganism and profligacy!

In my travels through the South, I often met Irish men and women whom riches, or long exposure to Protestant society, led to ignore the faith of their Fatherland—even good

Catholics would sometimes feel ashamed to recognize a Priest in a Protestant community. But the Irish servant girl, to my knowledge, was never ashamed to salute " the Priest," or acknowledge her faith. On the contrary, she felt as though the very room which the Priest or Bishop occupied in the hotel, was made sacred by his presence ; and often, by the simple act of placing wild flowers, or choice fruit on the centre-table ; or as she knelt at his feet for a blessing, revealed the little Irish world of faith and affection that dwelt in her heart.

When I stated that Priests were sometimes bound in Charity to take charge of money, jewelry, deeds, &c., of the departed, I should also have added the occasional necessity of his writing out a last " will " or " testament," and the advisability of his becoming guardian for children having "*means*," but bereft of friends.

For several months after the Fevers of '73 and '78, the pastors of Memphis had to be almost every week in court ; some with applications to become Guardians or Administrators; others appeared as testamentary witnesses, or the representatives of minors whose property was mortgaged or claimed by alleged creditors. This, of all the Priest's duties, is the most undesirable. For the benefit of younger brethren in the ministry, I would state that, unless where Justice or Charity make it obligatory, a Priest should never assume the responsibility of "guardian" or "executor." I would willingly undergo the labors of another Epidemic, rather than be repeatedly summoned to court, obliged to swear to all "audits," "outlays," and "deposits;" besides, procuring bondsmen, and often incurring the grudge or suspicion of the relatives and friends of the parties concerned. However, as some very serious difficulties occurred after the Fever, in regard to "wills" not properly attested or illegally drawn out, every clergyman should know how to write one, or at least have a copy of a legal "form," in order to preclude the possibility of future litigation.

As I have heretofore related several instances of heroism and self-sacrifice on the part of the laity, I trust it will not be out of place to relate an instance or two concerning the clergy in their devotion to their sacred calling and the cause of suffering humanity.

Of the Priests who died in '73, I have already stated, four belonged to the "Order" of St. Dominic, and one to that of St. Francis. The Provincial of the Dominican "Order" keenly felt the loss of such young and promising men. Still, having a house of his "Order" in Memphis, he felt it a duty incumbent upon him to fill up all vacancies.

FATHER J. D. SHEEHY, O. P.

During the autumn of '73, there was a venerable ex-Dominican Priest, named Father J——, residing in Nashville. He wore a long white beard, and was in appearance a veritable Patriarch. The good Father had already reached in years the scriptural term, threescore-and-ten. Although I will not vouch its accuracy, at all events, this story I heard repeatedly ; and it occasioned a good deal of mirth amongst the clergy living at the time. After the deaths of Fathers Cary, and O'Brien, the Provincial wrote to this old gentleman (according to the story), asking him if he would not be willing to leave Nashville and go to Memphis. The poor old man, having gleaned the contents of this ominous missive, with tear-fraught eyes, handed the letter to the Bishop. Archbishop P. A. Feehan, being then Bishop of Nashville, and the soul of kindness himself, naturally smiled at what rather seemed a joke, than a serious request. The old Priest, being very deaf, leaned over to hear the Bishop confirm his death-warrant. In his loudest effort, the Bishop said, "Don't mind, Father J——." "Must I go?" asked the deaf man. "No! Remain with me for the present." was the kind reply. It was wise of the Bishop not to send this old man. Being enfeebled by age, and incurably deaf, he could be of little or no assistance to the Yellow Fever sufferers. Besides, this good Priest had already served a "*golden Jubilee*" in the Ministry, and was one of the leading "Pioneers" of old Kentucky.

The story goes on to say that the Bishop wrote to the Provincial, and intimated that, unless he could find some younger and more useful Priest to send to Memphis, he would be obliged to provide one himself. Accordingly, the Provincial sent word to Louisville, where there was a branch house of the "Order." The Prior of this convent did not wish to command, or rather pass sentence of sure and speedy death on any of his brother Priests. He simply suggested that all should draw lots. If our Lord himself was agonized at the approach of death, we may naturally suppose that it was with tremulous hands, each slowly drew the straw which was to decide his mortal destiny. But when all had drawn—who held the fatal straw? Was it a young and vigorous man. or some enfeebled veteran, like Father J——? My informant assured me it was the oldest Priest in the community that was the unfortunate prizetaker. In a moment, this Patriarch made up his mind to face the battle. But he was mistaken, if he supposed for a moment that he would be allowed to go. From the ranks of the young Priests there stepped forward one of nature's noblemen, with as true a heart as ever beat within a martyr's breast. "Father C——, you shall not go," he said. "I will take your place." He then besought the Prior's permission, and took the train for Memphis that very evening.

A few days after, I saw that young Priest on his sick bed, prostrated with Fever. The "Fathers," the week previous, had just moved into their new convent. Although having some thirty rooms, Father S—— was the only occupant of the building. His brother Priest, Father Kelly (since dead), was at the time engaged attending sick calls. The sick Priest told me he was hungry, and that he would be glad to have some soup. My first thought was to request the Dominican Sisters to attend him from La Salette Academy; but I soon learned that they were nearly all stricken down, and had not sufficient attendance themselves. I then applied to a rich Catholic lady who lived next door. This ever-good and generous woman promised to do, and did, all in her power, but it would seem her services were too late. The good Priest must have been several hours without medicine, food or drink. Two days after, myself and a brother Priest called to see our patient, Father Sheehy. He did not sit up this time to greet us with his genial smile and firm grasp of the hand. No! The good Priest was dead. His face was calm, as the rays of the sun beamed over it, while his lips and teeth were stained with blood. He seemed as though he had come out of a bloody battle, after heaving a last sigh of relief and final victory.

Alban Butler, in his lives of the Saints, relates many touching and edifying examples of the faith and christian heroism of the martyrs of the primitive church, but the self-sacrificing Priest that lay on his cold and neglected bed that morning,—far away from parents and friends—deserves, I verily believe, to be classified among the foremost martyr-heroes of heaven. A thousand miles away, in New England, this Priest had a host of relatives and friends (Newport and Providence), who mourned his untimely death, and who now venerate all that is left to them—his picture in crayon and canvas. He was born in the parish of Graignamana, Co. Kilkenny, Ireland, in the year 1834: died Oct. 17, 1873.

### DR. LUKE BLACKBURNE.

In the autumn of '73, Dr. Luke Blackburne, then a physician of Louisville, but afterwards Governor of Kentucky, volunteered his services to aid the sufferers of Memphis during the Yellow Fever epidemic. He adopted homœopathy in his treatment, and to his credit, it must be said, he was remarkably successful. Although a Protestant, it is further due to him to say that, of all the physicians of Memphis, he was the only one who offered to perform the Cæsarean operation, in order that baptism might be administered to the unborn infant, when the mother was dead or in a desperate condition.

Although I only remember to have called the Doctor to one case of this kind, his "willingness" is worthy of Catholic recognition, especially when contrasted with the squeamish conduct of physicians, who, either positively refused, or ignored such a christian obligation. And here I make bold to state that, during and after the Fever, unborn infants might have been not only validly baptized, but artificially brought to the world, if physicians had, what few seemed to have, a christian conscience. Their shallow sympathy in favor of the mother often led them to deprive a human being of that dual life which God destined for it. We need not recur to the case of Cæsar, born after the death of his mother; the medical works of these professionals clearly demonstrate, not only the possibility, but, frequently, the *feasibility* of this operation. For this reason, I wish to call attention to the "large-mindedness" of Dr. Blackburne, as also to his philanthropy, which was not always confined to marble halls and telephone calls. Although I may have occasion to give him a few after "touches" of criticism, before I wind up his medical merits, I must say he never flinched from the calls of the poor and needy. At his invitation, I often travelled with him in his buggy through the different wards of North Memphis. Once, I had occasion to witness his "caning" dexterity. In one of the leading drug stores on Main street, he saw a gentleman whom he recognized, a rival physician. He directly accused him of disregarding the rules of medical courtesy, by interfering with his practice. Not receiving satisfactory answers, with his cane, he belabored his opponent on the head and shoulders. He challenged him to produce a diploma, and denied that he ever received one, and ended by saying he was nothing more than an old "Preacher."

Whatever might be said for or against Dr. Blackburne's botanic knowledge of physics, his physical ability, in this case, was beyond question. Amongst the Doctor's many patients were a family of the name of Sullivan. The entire household (twelve,) took the Fever. They all died except one little girl about ten years old. The Doctor, it would seem, saw this a grand occasion to surprise his many friends in Louisville, as, also, a living advertisement of his heroism and philanthropy in Memphis. Accordingly, he told little Mary Sullivan, for that was the child's name, that he was going to buy her some fine dresses, and take her with him to Louisville. Although I do not distinctly remember whether the Doctor made the flattering promise, at all events, it was the general gossip in the neighborhood that Mary was to be brought up a lady; sent to a first-class boarding school, and decently portioned for life. One of the girl's relatives told me the child was preparing to leave, and that the Doctor had already ordered her some very nice dresses. As Doctor Blackburne had been heretofore a comparative stranger to me, I forbade the child to leave until I could ascertain a certainty of his respectability. Although the pitiless hand of death had taken away all but the last one of the Sullivans, still the little surviving waif that was to represent the name seemed to have inherited all the mettle and faith of her departed family. When the Doctor brought his buggy to Mary's house, she appeared on the stoop and addressed him:— "Go away. I shan't go with you. The Priest told me he did not know you." The Doctor, admiring the child's *pluck*, in suppressed hilarity, demanded his dresses back again. "No, you shan't have them. Who asked you to give them?" Seeing there was no chance of getting little Mary to leave the city by persuasive or legal means, the Doctor drove down to see me in the parsonage. I had, after enquiries, been thoroughly satisfied as to his respectability; however, I told him it was only on condition he would send the child to a Catholic Seminary, that I would consent to let him take her. He agreed to this, and took the child to Louisville. The little waif was carried around to all his medical and merchant friends. Columns of free newspaper notoriety kept the Doctor and his little ward before the public eye for several days. At last, when sentiment and excitement began to wane, the Doctor, according to promise, sent little Mary Sullivan to the Sisters of Charity, Nazareth Academy. She remained there as a first class boarder for five years. You are now disposed to consider Dr. Blackburne a noble fellow—well, I think so, too— but little Mary Sullivan has a different opinion. The last time I met her, six years ago, she said, "The old thing never paid the poor Sisters a cent for me." "Who clothed you while in the Seminary?" I interposed. "Why, the Sisters, Father." Mary was then working in a laundry in Nashville, while Dr. Luke Blackburne was Governor of all Kentucky.

As the Doctor was most obliging and friendly to me during the Fever, I do not wish to cast any slur on his conduct for not paying Miss Sullivan's pension while at Nazareth Academy. It would appear there was no definite agreement on the part of the Doctor to pay for her at the Seminary. As a Protestant, I suppose he thought it enough to give her in charge of the Sisters. In truth, I would never consent to let him take the child if I did not believe she was to be educated and portioned for life. In my anxiety to have the child so well provided for, I may have overestimated the Doctor's promise. At all events, he did the child no injustice—recalling an epitaph I once saw on an old tombstone:

> "He did no harm, nor yet much good,
> And would have been better if he would."

Besides poor Mary Sullivan, other Yellow Fever waifs are scattered throughout various parts of the country. Some three or four whom I can recall have been sent to their grand-parents in Ireland. There are others in New York, Boston and Philadelphia. Here, in Providence, are five accomplished young ladies, (Roche,) whose parents had to battle with the Fever of '73. Three, (Mary, Annie and Maggie), have taken the white veil of the Order of Mercy; while the other two having likely a similar vocation, are studying at Bay View Seminary. In the Franciscan Convent, Joliet, Ill., are two Sisters (*nee* Foley) whose parents died in '73. A few waifs have gone astray, and ignored the faith of their fathers, but it is consoling to know they were only *few.* The Priests and Sisters were as jealous in their care of the living as of the departing souls. The people of Memphis, I must say, without any mitigated qualification, would be VERY ungrateful if they ever forget or fail to appreciate their labors in these tearful and trying days.

It is true there was, during all the plagues that visited Memphis, a society that did much good in its own way. The Howards, called after a philanthropist of the name, first organized themselves as a benevolent association during the summer of '73. Their avowed duties were to visit the sick, provide nurses, and assist the poor of every creed and color while the plague should last. They appealed to Masonic fraternities and the country at large, and by the funds they received from abroad and collected at home, were enabled to do a vast amount of good. But here, I must say that, as the members of the Howard Association were mostly all non-Catholics, the poor Irish were in too many instances either overlooked, or positively refused. Father W. Walsh, in page six of his Yellow Fever pamphlet, speaking of the Howards said: "The Howard Association (FOR AWHILE) honored my requisitions for nourishment for those sick of the Fever in the city. The citizens' relief gave us hard rations for about one-fifth of our people. * * * * * * It also gave a few boxes of ill-assorted clothing and two small supplies of delicacies for the sickly."

I remember, myself, attending a Magdalen in a Main street den in '73. (These unfortunate creatures were wofully decimated.) While hearing the girl's confession I was interrupted by the loud steps of a gentleman coming up stairs. For obvious reasons I shall not state to which Committee or Association he belonged. Addressing the lady by name, "Miss Lucy, can I do anything for you to-day?" She negatively shook her head. "Do you need coal, meat, medicine, nurse, tea?" He wound up by asking if there was anything in the way of *wine* he could send her. To all his questions she motioned a negative reply. And so well she might. This spotted dove slept in a carved walnut couch; a rich Brussels carpet, a piano, and other costly furniture adorned the room. On the floor lay scattered promiscuously a countless variety of bottles. Being somewhat piqued at the unceremonious interruption, in an angry tone, I spoke, in substance: "Since you have enumerated this catalogue of unappreciated dainties, I wish you would attend to a poor starving Irish family in Front street, who has been for several days begging your Committees, not for the luxuries, but the necessaries of life." His reply was sarcastic and very insulting. I threatened that if he failed, I would report his conduct and have it published in the daily papers. I went to re-visit this poor family next day. My words had effect; they received cart-loads of coal, blankets and provisions. This, and similar examples, should afford a lesson to Catholics never to send money during a famine or Fever, except through the supervision of the Bishop or Pastor. Sending it through, or to Societies or self-constituted Committees, no matter of what name or initials is, at best but a doubtful disbursement. In too many cases it never reaches the intended object.

## MATTIE STEVESON.

As the people, after a battle, plague, or pestilence, are sure to have a hero or a heroine, so, after the Fever of '73, the Howards, finding no special hero amongst themselves, selected a handsome-faced young lady (a volunteer nurse) for a Yellow Fever heroine. Her name was Mattie Steveson. She left her parents in Illinois, to come to Memphis, for the purpose of ministering to the wants of the sick and poor, if you will, or perhaps for the sake of earning ten dollars a day, the wages generally given to white nurses at that time. The monument raised to her memory in Elmwood cemetery would do honor to the remains of a princess. I happened to be in Walthal Infirmary the morning she died. A number of ladies were busily engaged making floral crosses, anchorets, and wreaths to adorn the casket. In her hands were placed a fragrant bouquet of virgin-white lilies, while all around her corpse and casket were strewn a profusion of fresh natural flowers. She was evidently a heroine,—at least with the Howards. Yet there were people in Memphis at the time, who considered Miss Steveson quite an ordinary woman: people who never saw or surmised anything in her young life or actions that would entitle her to this extraordinary " Beatification."

A respectable merchant of Front street told me Mattie nursed himself and wife for five days. He was obliged to send her away, for the reason she was generally absent when most needed, and that, like many of her sex, her winsome and best attentions were devoted to the looking-glass. But "*Nihil de mortuis, nisi bene.*" "Nothing of the dead but what is good." We do not grudge this young woman the unwonted praise she received from the citizens of Memphis, but if christian charity bids us speak well, and, when possible, hide the faults of the dead, even-handed Justice requires that we must not exaggerate personal qualities, or mistake common-place duty for undaunted heroism. Even if Miss Steveson had the desire, I doubt she possessed the faculty, while it is certain she had not the opportunity of doing anything extraordinary. All the patients she attended did not exceed five or six, most of whom paid her well for her services. This young woman did not half the benevolent work of the weakest Dominican or Franciscan Sister. Those creatures received no pay for their services, and were incessantly working night and day. Yet those of them who fell victims were taken to their graves, not in a silver-mounted casket, like Mattie Steveson, but in some improvised, unvarnished box,—no flowers on their sable

veils, no stone to mark the place where their
ashes repose. I do not wish to say or insinuate there was anything unladylike in her conduct; in fact, she would appear excessively
genteel—a qualification which is not always
the best for a sick room. In the room adjacent to that wherein Miss Steveson died, lay
the lifeless "remains" of a poor Irishwoman,
who, after nursing and burying her husband
and three children, volunteered her services
to the Howard Infirmary. No busy handmaids weaving chaplets cast their shadows in
the sunlight, which gleamed over her pallid
features. But this poor woman was neither
young nor very handsome—two qualifications
necessary for Masonic or modern beatification.
This good matron's "remains" were consigned
to a Potter's grave, while many of the young
"braves" of Memphis were making love to,
if not lots of money by, Miss Steveson's picture.

## UNDERTAKER JACK.

I shall pass over the events of '73, after
relating one other reminiscence, which I trust
will compensate for the time and space it shall
occupy.

During the Fever of '73, and indeed through
all the plagues that visited Memphis since it
rose to be an important city, there was an

undertaker in the city, whom I shall only designate by his christian name, John, or Jack, as he was more familiarly called. It is far beneath my purpose to expose this gentleman to contempt or ridicule. On the contrary, I consider him one of the most genial, charitable, and good-natured Irishmen in Memphis. It would be well if the Irish Catholics of Memphis could boast of many such men. If his outward physique is not remarkable for any special traits of symmetry, he carries within him a big heart, and a store of patience, capable of defying any zone on the earth's surface. As I had occasion to meet this man almost every week for nine years, I shall take the liberty of describing his appearance, and a few of his peculiarities.

While in weight and bulk he was competent, in height he was somewhat below the average. He wore long, very black whiskers, and bushy hair, with a moderate stoop to his shoulders. His countenance was severe and pale; in fact, so ghastly pale that it was often said Jack drove many a corpse whose face and looks would entitle him to "undertake," rather than be "undertaken" by this doughty little Knight of the "pall." Indeed, I often felt a chilly sensation myself, as the hearse slowly approached, with Jack, in tall hat and clerical costume, sitting between the plumes. Shrouded death is awe-inspiring at all times, but it seemed to reach the climax of solemnity only when Jack was in "position." If nature ever designed any one for this "grave" business, this man unquestionably possessed all the sable requisites. Other undertakers left no impression as to the christianity or creed of the "departed." From their business-like and unceremonious haste, it was impossible to distinguish a Christian from a Pagan funeral. Jack created a different and definite impression. His face, revealing the state of grace and gravity of the dead, reminded the mourners that now, indeed, the last corporal work of mercy was being solemnized. In appearance, as well as christian profession, Jack was conscientiously orthodox. To his further credit, it must be said, that, although professionally engaged with those to be consigned to another world, he seldom failed to recognize a friend, especially an Irishman. From his "elevated" position, no gentleman could doff his hat with more obsequience, whenever he passed a Priest or Catholic Sister on the street.

Towards the end of the Fever, there was a suppressed rumor that not only Jack, but several other undertakers who had not half his patronage, buried several patients alive.* I do not consider this remark worthy of serious notice; yet I feel obliged to state, many of the deceased were buried too soon after death. If we judge from the fact that the county undertaker buried 2500 bodies in less than ninety days, it is hard to blame them for this otherwise profane haste: and especially in those cases where Jack or his professional brethren expected to lose, or at most, to realize but little profit, it may be considered a pardonable exercise of the "craft" if they should bend a limb or dislocate a toe. During such wholesale carnage, it appeared natural to entertain the selfish view that the body should fit the coffin, not the coffin the body. A shoemaker and tailor differ in the fact that they must suit their customers, while the *customers* must suit the undertakers, if not, they will soon bring them to a state of subordination. In doing this, they are morally certain there will be no recrimination on the part of those "accommodated." In saying "morally certain," I leave room for those weird stories which speak of the dead as appearing entirely dissatisfied with their last consignment, and make them appear in the

---

* During the Cholera which preceded the Fever of '73 I met an acquaintance, whom I saluted, on the street (Winchester), about eight o'clock in the morning. About half past twelve I was called to his bedside, where I anointed him. This man died of Cholera and was buried before six the evening of the same day.

darkness of night, and sometimes in broad day-light, before the men who neglected to give them decent christian interment. No matter what pleasantries are related at Jack's expense, he is sure to smile and take them in good part; he often encourages, and sometimes tells very good things himself regarding some of his posthumous experience. Indeed, if all the ludicrous things said of Jack were true, it would be hard to recriminate him, at least during this awful time, when, to use his own words: "Business was very brisk."

Before the year 1873 Memphis was remarkably healthy. To the question: "How are times?" Jack would invariably answer: "*Dull*, very dull times." When seventy or one hundred "Stiffs" had to be put under ground every day, business was considered "brisk" in undertaking parlance. The Priests attached to St. Bridget's Church in 1873 had each an average of one hundred sick calls a day. Of these, 90 per cent fell victims during the first month or six weeks. During such wholesale slaughter it would be hard to censure Jack if he tolerated or connived at a little unceremonious manipulation in his profession. It is done in every trade, and perhaps no one knows better than Jack himself that the craft practised on the living does far greater violence to humanity than any "after touch" of his economy. Jack was not only a necrologist, but was even brave and charitable.

The parents of a family named H—— died during the rage of the Fever (in '73). They left five children. Whenever such cases occurred, the Priests or Sisters had to look after the children immediately, lest they should be sent to the Protestant Asylums, or taken away by parties from whom they could not be again recovered. Such disposition of children after the demise of the parents explains, to some extent, the fact of Methodist, Baptist and Episcopal ministers in the South having such Celtic names as Hickey, Murphy, McAvoy, etc. In '73, there was an Episcopal minister by the name of Patrick O'Neil, living in Covington, Tenn.; and in Osceola, Arkansas, a Baptist preacher by name Thomas Quinn.* One or two years for children in a Protestant orphanage, or with a Protestant family, will suffice to jeopardize their faith; while in too many instances apostate men and women have lost the faith in this way. Returning to the H —— children. While I was endeavoring to bring them together, in order to send them to the Sisters' orphan asylum, some disreputable persons living in the rear

---

*In 1886, there was in Memphis a minister (Christian) named Rev. G. W. Sweeney.

part of the house concealed the two larger girls. As I entered the house, where I supposed they were secreted, a vicious looking man and two young girls impeded my approach. One of the latter, holding a fence lath, declared with an oath she would have my life if I advanced one step farther. Having no desire to test her "fencing" ability, I considered it prudent to leave the premises, but with a firm determination to rescue the children before they would spend one night where they were. During my search for the children, an immense crowd was attracted to the scene, not one of whom, however, attempted to interfere. At a distance, I descried Jack, with his iron-gray and natty buggy. I motioned him to come up. Advancing, he drove at a furious speed, thinking, perhaps, he had another corpse. I explained how things were, and told him to drive up town and bring a policeman. He jumped into his buggy and started immediately. He had gone about six blocks when he returned in an awful heat of excitement. As he had an impediment in his speech, it took him a few seconds to distinctly articulate. "Fa–Fa–Father, I fo–fo–forgot—I, I, I'm an Alderman—have the pow–pow–power of a policeman; what do you want me to do?" "To break or force that door open."

The little man took hold of an axe and gave the door one vigorous blow that smashed it open in splinters. He defied the virago, secured the children, and did meritorious work that day. With the boys of the City Council, the joke was that Jack had gone six blocks before he ever remembered he was an Alderman. Would that every Alderman made such good use of his municipal prerogatives as Jack!

# THE YELLOW FEVER SCOURGE
## OF 1878.

Only a few months had elapsed since the Fever of '73, when the people began to take courage. Trade, commerce, and labor seemed to have gained their former prestige. Real estate and stocks not only appeared to have outlived, but really to have attained more stability after their recent depression. Whole blocks that were labelled "For Sale," "For Rent," were now crowded with mercantile goods of every description. Every consecutive year saw the erection of scores, if not hundreds of private residences, stores, and warehouses. The clamorous noise of the foundry; the hissing and boom of the cotton-press; the shrill or hoarse scream of the locomotive or steamboat, showed the city was alive to business of every department. Cotton bales, piled mountains high on either side of the principal thoroughfares—Front, Main, Second streets—sometimes almost a mile in length, showed that the farmer was not idle in his contribution to the wealth of Memphis.

The churches, too, were in keeping with the progress of the times. A new and splendid edifice was erected for the Catholics of Fort Pickering by the energy of Rev. A. Luiselli, a devoted Priest, who did noble work during the late epidemic. Towards the spring of '78, Memphis was not merely convalescent, but appeared almost entirely recuperated from her ancient disasters. But Providence, it seems, had not yet laid aside the "chastening rod." At the very time when the people began to regard "Fever" as an irrevocable spectre of the past, it stalked forth a dread reality. Those citizens who thought God had ceased to visit them in wrath, found they were wofully mistaken. If old wiseacres attributed the wrath of God in '73 to the shameful and Godless celebration of Mardi Gras, they were in a hopeless quandary now, since this Pagan custom had been long since abolished.

If the Fever of '73 were sometimes called a plague, that of '78 was a veritable scourge. Father Wm. Walsh, in his pamphlet of '78, writing for aid to the various temperance unions of America, describes the condition of affairs: "Out of a population of 45,000 or 50,000 inhabitants, 35,000 or 40,000 have fled for their lives when the plague broke out. Of the 8,000 or 10,000 who remained, over 7,000 are reported as having been stricken down by the Fever. The county undertaker has a registry of 2,500 burials by himself alone. * * * The bravest and noblest of every rank were being daily stricken down, and their remains hurriedly carried away to the various cemeteries or the Potter's field. Those of us whom God was pleased to spare, in order to administer to the wants of the sick, the needy, and the dead, had to witness scenes which pen cannot describe, and to undergo labors which, on some occasions at least, might be considered superhuman. Among our Sisters and Priests, the Fever made great havoc. Almost a score of Sisters died. Of the Priests who were in the city when the Fever broke out, only three of us escaped. * * * * Physicians and nurses, as yet, know no specific remedy for Yellow Fever patients. It is a fact that, wherever the disease was directly attacked by the powers of medicine, the life of the patient was directly attacked." This prolonged quotation gives the views of a young Priest, who was most active, and who has attended, if not more, at least as many, patients as any of the clergy that lived through the Fever that year.

As the late Rev. A. J. Ryan, deservedly called the Poet-Priest of the South, for his unflinching adhesion to the "Southern Cause," had been a special favorite with the people of

Memphis, to whom, in one of his last lectures, he said, "We fought for our *rights,* and we *were right,*" I presume his poem on the Yellow Fever Epidemic of 1878 will be read with interest.

>Purer than thy own white snow,
>  Nobler than thy mountain's height;
>Deeper than the ocean's flow,
>  Stronger than thy own proud might:
>Oh! Northland to thy sisterland,
>Was late thy Mercy's generous deed and grand.
>
>Nigh twice ten years the sword was sheathed;
>  Its mist of green o'er battle plain
>For nigh two decades spring had breathed;
>  And yet the crimson life-blood stain
>From passive swards had never paled,
>Nor fields, where all were brave and some had failed.
>
>Between the Northland, bride of snow,
>  And Southland, brightest sun's fair bride,
>Swept, deepening ever in its flow,
>  The stormy wake, in war's dark tide:
>No hand might clasp across the tears,
>And blood and anguish of four deathless years.
>
>When summer, like a rose in bloom,
>  Had blossomed from the bud of spring,
>Oh! who could deem the dews of doom
>  Upon the blushing lips could cling?
>And who could believe its fragrant light
>Would e'er be freighted with the breath of blight?
>
>Yet o'er the Southland crept the spell,
>  That e'en from out its brightness spread;
>And prostrate, powerless, she fell,
>  Rachel like, amid her dead.
>Her bravest, fairest, purest, best,
>The waiting grave would welcome as its guest.

The Northland, strong in love, and great,
  Forgot the stormy days of strife;
Forgot that souls, with dreams of hate,
  Or unforgiveness, e'er were rife
Forgotten was each thought, and hushed;
Save—she was generous, and her foe was crushed.

No hand might clasp from land to land;
  Yea, there was one to bridge the tide,
For at the touch of Mercy's hand,
  The North and South stood side by side:
The bride of snow, the bride of sun,
In charity's espousals are made one.

"Thou givest back my sons again,"
  The Southland to the Northland cries:
"For all my dead on battle plain
  Thou biddest my dying now uprise:
I still my sobs, I cease my tears,
And thou hast recompensed my anguished years"

Blessings on thine every wave;
  Blessings on thine every shore;
Blessings that from sorrow save,
  Blessings giving more and more,
For all thou gavest thy sisterland,
Oh! Northland, in thy generous deed, and grand.

The virulency Fever of '78, from the death of Butler P. Anderson* (29th of August), prevailed until the end of November, '79. Mr. Pat. Ryan, sexton of St Bridget's church, and his cousin, Mr. P. Mackey, after an absence of three months, returned to the city, when both took the Fever and died 21st November. The Fever had already taken hold during the latter part of July, and was

---

* Keating's Yellow Fever History states that Mrs. Zack died of Fever on the 5th of August, and her brother-in-law also; Mrs. Bionda died Aug. 13, '78.

actually raging towards the middle of August, yet the Board of Health were loath to admit, and the city papers failed to announce the presence of Yellow Fever. 958 deaths, according to the *Memphis Appeal* of August, '78, had already occurred within the city limits before the Board of Health officially announced the Fever epidemic. Great God! I well remember the panic that almost crazed the populace the morning it was first announced in the papers. Men, women, and children, in wagons, street cars and carriages, all dashing through the streets on their way to the various railway depots and steamboat landings! The platforms of the L. & N.; the M. & C.; the Mem. & Tenn., and the Little Rock depots, were covered with mountains of trunks, boxes, and other portable furniture. All the trains that could be had were called into immediate action. In the short space of three days not less than thirty thousand people fled the city, going North, East, West—wherever they had friends—anywhere, from the ravages and reach of the Scourge. Each train had generally from fifteen to twenty passenger coaches attached. On some occasions, three locomotives were in requisition, two in front, and one in the rear, carrying their loads of human freight. All this is not hearsay, but facts witnessed by my own eyes.

The cars, during the exodus, were so crowded that several women and children fainted from pressure and exhaustion. Some were bruised or suffocated beyond recovery. In two or three instances a conductor assured me that mothers, while in the cars, gave birth to premature babes. Drink and provisions were nowhere to be obtained. As a train stopped before a tank to take water, (Humboldt) a young man jumped off the train and succeeded in bringing a bucket of water. The thirst was so great that he readily received a dollar for every glass he was willing to dispense. Even at this price, hundreds failed to get it. Father O'Brien, at present residing in Chicago, assured me that he did not taste a morsel of food or drink for twelve hours he was in the train. Even then, in response to a telegram addressed to a friend on the road, he only succeeded in getting a few crusts of bread and a glass of water, while the train took water at the tank. No train was allowed to stop at any station nearer than Louisville, 396 miles. Even there, the trains were obliged to remain some considerable distance outside the city limits. The smaller towns on the different railroads for two hundred miles outside Memphis, and a similar distance above and below Memphis on the river, were so strict in quarantine regulations that pickets, cordoned all round each town, had imperative orders to prevent all men, women and children from entering their corporation limits. In case any one violated their remonstrance, they were empowered to shoot him dead. A Lady, after walking from Humboldt to Jackson (19 miles), encountered the pickets as she approached the latter city. They ordered her back under penalty of death. The poor woman was obliged to retrace her steps; a few days after, she was found dead near the railroad. On another occasion while the train stopped to take water at Humboldt, an Irish school-teacher, (just landed from Ireland) got off the train. He had to walk eleven miles to Milan, the next station. Here, the Fever that must have been in his system, developed. He was taken outside the town, and put into a freight box-car, where he was left to die, and where he actually perished, either from starvation or disease, no human being having courage enough to approach him. In fact, it was a mortal risk for any one to visit him.

A Priest who called on a number of Fever patients at Grand Junction, was shunned as if he were an evil spirit. He found it the most difficult task to obtain a little bread and some milk. As the train did not leave till next day he was obliged to sleep under the Sanctuary carpet, although the night,

(November) was very cold. City guards, Preachers, and Inkeepers, all gave him a wide berth as he approached. This same Priest gave another awful scare to the citizens of an adjacent town. A brother Priest called to see him on his return from Memphis. After two days' sojourn, a virulent case of small pox developed in the person of his guest. All at once the city got into a blaze of excitement. Two policeman were stationed at the door on guard, day and night. The Protestant element demanded that the young Priest should be taken outside the city limits. The Catholics would not consent. This occurred in Jackson, Tenn. The meat, bread, vegetables and medicines required were cautiously laid on the front door-steps. The poor Priest, Father John Walsh, died. After his death the parsonage was almost entirely depleted—carpets, bed, bedding,—all destroyed, without any remuneration for their loss. A neighboring resident further assured me they even broke and burnt his stove. This city-scaring Priest, to whom I have recently referred, owing to ill health has left the diocese of Nashville, and is now the Pastor of a flourishing parish in Lake View, Chicago, (Father P. O'Brien.)

Although this last narration is a digression from the subject of Yellow Fever, I thought it would be interesting in so far as it shows how excitable and scary the Southern country people are, especially when an emissary of the Pope is in the vicinage. But while cholera and small pox have terrors for the young, and especially the beautiful, the weird and ghastly presence of Yellow Fever is shunned alike by young and old, "white" and "colored."

### THE MUCH-ABUSED, BUT VERY SENSIBLE IRISH-MAN, JOHN D——.

I remember staying over night at a hotel in a village called Brownsville, sixty miles from Memphis. The famous railroad contractor, John D—— was also there at the time. It was then I brought him the sad news of the death of his wife, who, with her children had taken the Fever. John was singled out by the papers and the citizens of Memphis at large, as being a heartless coward for not going in to see his dying wife and sick children. I would undertake to apologize for John's action at the time. In the first place, as he tearfully admitted to myself, he could do them no good. Then again in the event of his children surviving (they did survive) his going to Memphis would deprive them of a father in addition to the loss they had already sustained. Yellow

Fever had an insatiate rapacity for such giants; and John, who with his keen eye could grade a railroad bed or securely fasten a cross tie, saw this patent fact. Take his dilemma into calm consideration. One horn pointed to his dying wife and three children in Memphis; the other, which was John's favorite, pointed to himself, still a young and healthy man, in the enjoyment of wealth and security in Brownsville. A greater man than John—Hamlet—after debating a long time with himself, decided that "To be" was better than "not to be." If John went to Memphis that time and died he would get a great deal of free newspaper notoriety and, perhaps, be immortalized as a hero. But, like a wise man, he feared that perhaps he would not be in a position to read those accounts with any zest of social enjoyment. This good man concluded it was better to keep away from the worms as long as he could. Good reader, which side would common sense and prudence dictate to yourself?

There is, I admit, a good deal of daring resolve to be seen among quadrupeds; but take the average *biped*, especially that individual called *man*, and I warrant you will find him if not nervously cautious, at least exceedingly careful when old grim death is taking his inventory. Positive facts are stubborn things in Mr. D——'s favor. Had he gone to Memphis during the fair autumn of '78, he would have been a negative creature for the past seven years. Worse than that—his children, whom he has ever since decently supported and educated, would be homeless—perhaps penniless waifs.

The young wives and sentimental ladies of Memphis all said John was a big coward. Making no objection to their estimation of his avoirdupois or cubic dimensions, (he was about six feet three in height and about 320 pounds weight,) I beg these fair ladies to be slow in condemning the man. While admitting there was plenty room for sentiment in John, I think he must be credited also for having a considerable amount of good solid sense. His conduct, I admit, touched the keenest part of conjugal nature—the willingness of the male to die for his mate—but I think a married man of sufficient ballast can overbear all these things, especially if he has a superior object in view. At all events it is a question which theologians may decide, whether a married man in safe grounds, and having a helpless family to support, is bound to see (not save) his dying wife and by so doing incur the risk of almost certain death. This was exactly the case of John D—— in '78. This poor, or rather rich and respectable man, was made the butt of lampoon; for several months after the Fever he dared not show his face in Memphis. Even churchmen joined in heaping coals of wrath and ridicule upon his head. With the ladies, he had no quarters at all. Perhaps a careful observer might see the tables of sentimentality turned against some of themselves in '78.

I remember seeing an aged widow so broken-hearted, so demented, so bereft at the death of her husband that it required four men to prevent her from throwing herself into the grave just after her husband's coffin was deposited. Would you believe? That woman was married again in three months after! That was an outburst of sentiment from first to last. It was Horace who said: "*Naturam, expellas furcâ, tamen usque recurrit.*" "You may turn nature out of doors with violence, but she will still return." Not a few of those cynic lady-connoisseurs who regarded John D—— as an untoward monster during the month of August, '78, in less than twelve months after regarded him as a dear little "package" of cardinal virtues.

Matrons of Memphis, do not take offence, for I do not mean to offer it when I say that many of you dear good creatures that moistened with your briny tears many a silk and embroidered handkerchief, mourning for your "dear departed" husbands, may now be occasionally seen in the ottoman-bestrewn parlor, or over the modest kitchen range, imprinting a soft or savage kiss on the forehead, or pointing an index into the dimple of some chubby little "cherub" that never saw, or will never care to see his dear departed *step-papa*. I have no recrimination for this. I would simply console you with a repetition of the words of Horace: "*Naturam expellas furcâ, tamen usque recurrit.*"

### EVENTS OF THE FEVER OF '78.

Having staid over night at a hotel, the morning I met Mr. Donovan, it leaked out that I was a Priest, and had come from Memphis. When I went to the desk to pay the inn-keeper for night's bed and board, he said he was sorry, but that he could not furnish me a room or allow me to stay any longer in the hotel. "Your presence here has ruined my house. All the boarders hearing that you had come from Memphis, have been leaving the house ever since midnight." After this I went over to an Irish family named Keeley, at whose residence I remained over night. The same day that I left Memphis a Miss Sullivan also left and staid several days at Keeley's. Keeley and his family took the Fever. He died, himself. From them it soon spread throughout the entire town and carried away some of the best citizens of the place. Although I left Memphis at the same time, Miss Sullivan was cautiously regarded as the individual who brought the Yellow Fever to Brownsville.

I now request the reader to accompany me back again to Memphis. In less than one week, out of a population of 65,000, there remained in the city but 19,600, of whom 14,000 were negroes. Of these, some eight hundred, a Howard encampment, some four miles outside the city, on the Hernando road; and about four hundred to Camp Father Mathew, located on the Hill, Fontaine farm, some three miles and a half from the city limits.

## CAMP FATHER MATHEW.

The establishment of this Camp was entirely due to the zeal and untiring energy of Rev. William Walsh. Its officers were members of the Father Mathew "Temperance Association," of which Father Walsh was spiritual director and President. Although Father Walsh, at the time, was but an assistant Priest at St. Patrick's, and had received but little encouragement in his scheme from the city Pastors, yet, on his own responsibility, he applied to the Secretary of War in Washington for tents and rations for his society and people. The Secretary honored his application, and in less than a week he received some seventy or eighty tents, capable of sheltering about four hundred persons. This Camp was a little prohibition city in itself. The use of intoxicants was strictly forbidden except as a prescribed medicine. Pickets were stationed around the Camp, with strict orders forbidding any one to enter or leave the grounds without the expressed permission of the President. The tents were pitched in such a manner that they formed streets, named after the Sacred Heart, Blessed Virgin, and other tutelar Saints, including Father Mathew and Father William. There could be no selection of site for camp purposes more eligible. In the midst of the farm, covering some two hundred acres, there was a boiling spring, surrounded by groves of forest trees; besides, its proximity to the city made it very convenient for the conveyance of provisions, while its isolation from Fever quarters rendered it perfectly safe and sanitary. But the most important institution of Camp Mathew was the little "Ark," wherein Mass was celebrated every morning. This Ark is yet intact, although transferred to St. Bridget's church. It has been, and ever will be, an object of veneration. Its cubic dimensions might be figured 10 x 8 x 8 feet. On the altar stood a beautiful statue of the Sacred Heart. The refugees of Camp Father Mathew placed entire confidence in the Sacred Heart, and to this day attribute their deliverance "to its Mercy and Merits."

It is, indeed, worthy of particular notice that, out of a population of 400 in the Camp, only ten died of Fever, and these cases were contracted in the city. Dr. Cavenagh, the attendant physician (since dead), declared that neither medical skill nor camp precautions, but Providence, saved the people of Camp Mathew. A few who left the Camp had sad reasons to believe this. Amongst the latter, was a noble-hearted fellow named Rollins. He had scarcely left the Camp when he took the Fever and died.

Besides the requisite number of sleeping tents, the Camp was composed of a commissary, a butchery, a drug shop, and a kitchen. During the sojourn of the Camp, some five babes were born, and two marriages took place. I had the privilege of solemnizing one of these, the contracting parties being Mr. Andrew Kelly and Miss Hanna Jones, both whose ages at the time would scarcely exceed thirty-six years. In order to reach the Camp that year, I had to travel by hand-car from Shelby to Memphis, a distance of eighteen miles. The Camp was mainly supported by the voluntary contributions of the Catholics throughout the United States. The average expenses amounted to $150 a day. During a period of ninety days, some thirty thousand dollars were received and disbursed to aid the camp-refugees, as also the suffering and poor of the city.

### PRIESTS WHO DIED OF YELLOW FEVER DURING THE EPIDEMICS OF 1873, '78 AND '79.

As I have not had an opportunity to obtain many detailed facts regarding the life of each, I trust my account, being entirely the result of personal acquaintance, if not cherished companionship, will prove interesting. And since I have not had an occasion to furnish the reader with a summary of the havoc death wrought amongst the clergy, I beg to preface the following general remarks : Besides some fifty Sisters, the diocese of Nashville lost twenty-two Priests, of whom twenty-one died in Memphis in less than five years. Of these, eight were secular, eight Dominican, and five Franciscan Fathers.

The following list gives the names, date of death, and age of each :

| NAME. | DIED. | AGED. |
|---|---|---|
| 1. Rev. J. R. DAILY, O. P. | Sept. 23, 1873 | 27 |
| 2. Rev. B. V. CARY, O. P. | Oct. 7, 1873 | 40 |

## PRIESTS WHO DIED OF YELLOW FEVER.

| NAME. | DIED. | AGED. |
|---|---|---|
| 3. Rev. D. A. O'BRIEN, O. P. | Oct. 9, 1873 | 42 |
| 4. Rev. J. D. SHEEHY, O. P. | Oct. 17, 1873 | 43 |
| 5. Rev. FATHER LEO, O. S. F. | Oct. 17, 1873 | 45 |
| 6. Rev. MARTIN WALSH | Aug. 29, 1878 | 40 |
| 7. Rev. J. A. BOKEL, O. P. | Aug. 29, 1878 | 29 |
| 8. Rev. J. R McGARVEY, O. P. | Aug. 29, 1878 | 33 |
| 9. Rev. MICHAEL MEAGHER | Aug. 30, 1878 | 46 |
| 10. Rev. FATHER ERASMUS, O. S. F. | Aug. 31, 1878 | 42 |
| 11. Rev. PATRICK McNAMARA | Sept 3, 1878 | 28 |
| 12. Rev. V. P. MATERNUS, O. S. F. | Sept. 9, 1878 | 35 |
| 13. Very Rev. MARTIN RIORDAN, V. G. | Sept. 17, 1878 | 46 |
| 14. Rev. P. J. SCANLON, O. P. | Sept. 19, 1878 | 30 |
| 15. Rev. V. B. VANTROOSTENBERG. | Sept. 19, 1878 | 35 |
| 16. Rev. J. J. MOONEY | Sept. 27, 1878 | 46 |
| 17. Rev. German FATHER, O. S. F. (ASIMUS). | 1878 | |
| 18. Rev. EDWARD DOYLE | Sept. 4, 1879 | 46 |
| 19. Rev. JOHN FAHEY | Sept. 6, 1879 | 29 |
| 20. Rev. V. G CHRYSOSTOM REINIKE, O. S F. | Sept. 9, 1879 | 39 |
| 21. Rev D. E. REVILLE, O. P. | 1879 | 39 |
| 22. Rev. PATRICK RYAN (Chattanooga). | 1878 | 38 |

The youngest of these Priests was but 27, and the oldest 50 years. Fourteen of the above named Priests were either born in Ireland, or of Irish parents; six were German, one French, and one Belgian. At the outbreak of the Fever, they all appeared to be robust, and remarkably healthy men. In the New York *Freeman's Journal* of '78, it was mentioned that, of all the Priests who died in Memphis, there was but one who possessed more than five dollars at the time of death. It is a fact known to the Catholics of Memphis that the secular clergy neither made nor had occasion to make a "will," disposing of coin, stocks, or real estate. In fact, the secular clergy who died of Fever did not leave "means" sufficient to liquidate the moderate dry goods and grocery bills that were presented to their successors for payment. Vicar General M. Riordan and Rev. M. Walsh, who had the two largest congregations in Memphis, did not own the weight of silver that covered their eyes in death.

Father P. McNamara sent me a telegram from his death-bed, with a view to settle a little monetary account that stood between us. Learning that it was impossible for me to comply with his request, the poor man "willed" me his library to reimburse for the "trifle" he had borrowed. His Breviaries are those which I use to this day. When Christmas comes round, I always feel sad to read over the title page of the "Nativity" these lines in original chirography: "Maggie wishes her *dearest brother* many, Oh! *very many* happy returns of this day."

I would cause the parishioners of St. Patrick's to smile were I to to insinuate that Father Doyle had money *before,* or left any *after* his death. I verily believe this Priest never laid aside for a future contingency the amount of five dollars from the day he was ordained until the day he died. As he entered, so he left the world, with nothing more valuable than his honest face and the vestments that clothed his meagre corpse. Father Mooney was the only Priest who had anything in the shape of greenbacks when he was called to give up his life. His estate will not excite much avarice when I inform the reader that he was but (up to the year of his death) Chaplain at the Christian Brothers' College, Memphis, having the modest salary of three hundred dollars a year. Before his death he bequeathed his little treasure, even his library, for Masses to be said for his soul after death. Father Meagher, who built a church in Edgefield that cost over $75,000, left after death no visible property except his gold watch and chain and his magnificent library. Father Fahey, when abroad, always wore an elegant suit of clothes, and at home a very neat cassock. If we except about fifty volumes and his breviaries, he left nothing else. Mr. Pat. O'Rourke, the redoubtable sexton of St. Peter's Church, could out-bid not only the Priests of Memphis in '78, but the whole clergy of the diocese of Nashville. In fact, he had a monetary claim on St. Patrick's church, which neither the Vicar General nor the two succeeding pastors found it possible to cancel. I trust it will not be taken as a revelation of church secrets to state that Very Rev. M. Riordan owed his niece seven hundred, and his books show that he had borrowed two thousand dollars from his sister, Mrs. Dr. Cogan, of St. Louis, Mo., which neither he nor his two successors could return.

In mentioning these facts, I disavow the purpose of casting odium on the Catholics of Memphis. In regard to their contributions towards the church, and their support of the clergy, they are not *second* to any people in America. When the people suffer the Priests must also suffer. When we consider the fact that several of the best parishioners of Memphis were swept away by the Fever; while others sold their homesteads and left the city, it will not be wondered at that the Priests not only died but lived Martyrs.

Although eight years have elapsed, Catholicity in Memphis has not yet recovered from the shock of the late Epidemics. Up to the year '78 there were always three Priests attending St. Patrick's, and two St. Bridget's Churches. At present, as the Directory will show, there is but one Priest at St. Patrick's and one at St. Bridget's.

While detailing the impecunious condition of the Memphis clergy, I did not, and do not wish to cast obloquy on those Priests who lay aside a moderate amount of money for a future contingency. Old age and sickness can, and often does lay a heavy hand on them. While children have their parents and husbands and wives, their mutual resources, the disabled or incapacitated Priest has seldom any one to offer him a helping hand. Besides, he should never be exposed to be anything approaching beggary. Considering the trifling salary that is allotted to Priests throughout Europe and America, I surmise it must be a *miserly* heart that will grudge them the little they can save after expenditures for clothing and judicious charity offerings. The laborer is worthy of his *wages*, and it is a vengeful sin to deprive him of it. A Priest who serves the Altar should live by the Altar. A protestant Preacher will get from two to five, while some receive ten thousand dollars yearly salary. Catholics who pretend to be very poor never hesitate to call a physician when sickness occurs. Every visit is generally charged two dollars. A book-keeper, grocery, or dry-goods clerk, in order to live decently must get at least a thousand dollars a year. This is more than many a Pastor's income, and assuredly no Assistant Pastor in any diocese of America receives such a liberal salary. I do violence to the dignity of the Priesthood in comparing their deserts with the income of the above-mentioned professionals. In every sense, physical, moral and intellectual, Priests are the foremost body of men in the world. A Priest one day in the confessional, effectually heals more immoral diseases than a physician could do in a lifetime. Besides, in educating a young man for the Priesthood, the parents and members of the family have often to strain their resources before his course is completed. In this country, I know several Priests whose college pensions were defrayed by their poor sisters working in dry goods firms, jewelry shops, or factories; while in Ireland, many a decent farmer's child, now in penury, would be in competent circumstances, were it not that the parents had to give all their saved income to keep their son in All-Hallows or Maynooth. Although I do not advocate Priests living or dying very rich, still, the people should know that they have a *right* to donate or keep what they *honestly earn*.

Asking the reader's pardon for this prolonged departure from the subject, I shall now detail a few of the virtues and qualities that adorned the life of the Memphis martyrs of '78 and '79.

### REV. MICHAEL MEAGHER.

Rev. Michael Meagher, the son of a respectable country farmer, residing one mile outside the limits of the town of Roserea, County Tipperary, Ireland, was born in or about the year 1832. He completed his theological course in Maynooth College, when (having attained the highest honors of the Dunboyne establishment) he soon after his ordination emigrated to this country. In New York he attached himself to the "Order" of Jesuits, in whose college at Fordham he distinguished himself as one of its leading Professors. He afterwards left the "Order" and came to Nashville, where he found his old friend and classmate, Right Rev. P. A. Feehan, Bishop of the diocese. Having remained with the Bishop at the Cathedral several years, where he became most conspicuous for the depth and eloquence of his sermons and lectures, he subsequently undertook to erect a church in East Nashville. As the limits of his new parish in Edgefield were not very extensive, he found it impossible to complete his gigantic undertaking by the united efforts of his parishioners. As failure was foreign to his nature, he resolved to call into action his natural resources, as also the generosity of his many clerical friends in the North and East. His erudite discourses and eloquence being known to the many thousands who heard him, it will be enough to add that by his lecturing tour he realized a sum bordering on seventy-five thousand dollars. As the church which he intended to erect would cost at least $150,000, it was sad to think the good Priest was not permitted to complete the object of his zeal and arduous labors.

In July, 1878, Father Meagher obtained a vacation to spend a few weeks in Memphis, with his cousin, Rev. Martin Walsh. While there, the Yellow Fever broke out in Memphis. Having returned from an adjacent mission (Covington), I warned Father Meagher of his danger, and requested him to let me take his place. With a cynic smile of disapproval, he answered, "No; I like to have a tussle with *Yellow Jack.*" Like a gallant son of Tipperary, he fought till he fell. After some three days' sickness, he died on the 30th of August, 1878. His first cousin, Father Walsh, had died in the next room a few hours previous. The two affectionate cousins are now lying beside each other in Calvary cemetery mound. On the gravestone over Father Meagher's head are the words, "*Vixit ut obiit.*" "He lived as he died." Little did those who heard this physical as well as intellectual giant lecture on the previous St. Patrick's day, imagine that those eyes, sparkling with patriotic fire, would so soon be dimmed and closed forever. The words that fell from his eloquent lips, like those of his great namesake, or another Mitchell, burnt deep conviction into the hearts of his audience. At present, there is a stained glass window erected to his memory in St. Bridget's church—a well-merited, if not a befitting tribute to the man who, while he might have left without any risk of reputation, preferred to die for the people of Memphis.

After his death, on his person were found a steel cincture and wristlets studded with iron spikes. These relics are still in the possession of Rev. William Walsh, present Pastor of St. Bridget's church.

This Priest, although but forty-six years of age at the time of his death, was favorably known and respected in almost every State of the Union. The Rev. Mother Superioress of the Ursuline Convent of Providence, as also several Priests and prominent merchants of New York, Philadelphia, Chicago and Montreal, are near relatives of his family.

### VERY REV. MARTIN RIORDAN, V. G.

Very Rev. M. Riordan was born near the city of Queenstown, County Cork, Ireland. From the age given at his death (50), he was born in the year 1828. He was ordained from Maynooth College, County Dublin, for the Archdiocese of St. Louis, Mo. When his friend, Rev. P. A. Feehan, was appointed Bishop of Nashville, he volunteered to accompany him to his new diocese, where he remained till his death, Sept. 17, 1878.

Bishop Feehan, appreciating his learning and talents, appointed him Vicar General of the diocese. It was acknowledged by all who knew him that he was a clergyman of superior knowledge, culture, and financial ability. He possessed far more sterling qualities than he avowed or professed; while those he impersonated were superlative. The glow of his genial smile; his kind and ever cheerful words, and the deeds of his large and generous heart, have not departed with his "remains." With all respect to those who have succeeded him, I feel convinced that the soul of the late Martin Riordan is the kindred and most beloved spirit in St. Patrick's parish to this day. Like the Shandon bells of his favorite city, the sound of his name is still music to the ears of his surviving flock. If his enfeebled health did not permit him assume all the duties of a zealous pastor, he more than compensated, not merely by his suave address, and priestly dignity, but in his acknowledged excellence in philological lore and philosophical profundity.

During the month of July, '78, Father Riordan was absent from the diocese, recuperating his health with some clerical friends in the East. Although after a severe attack of illness, he came right back to his parish as soon as he heard Yellow Fever had appeared in Memphis. While in his best health, his corpulent frame made it difficult, if not painful, to attend the sick, still, he went through lanes and alleys, from house to hut and hovel, on his godly mission. In this way, his exhausted strength gave out before he succumbed to the Fever. He was nursed to convalescence by the Josephite Sisters, when, by a fatal exposure in getting out of bed too soon, he relapsed, and never left his room again. His apparent recovery disappointed his many thousand friends in Memphis, who hoped and prayed that at least their beloved *Father Riordan* might be spared. Not only the parishioners, but the Priests of the diocese, looked up to this venerable man as a kind father and an ever true friend.

He was passionately devoted to the works of Addison, Johnson, Goldsmith and Scott. His language from the pulpit was so choice, and his knowledge of sacred and profane history so extensive, that the *elite* of the city, both Protestant and Catholic, flocked to hear him preach. His apprehension of the subject so affected his nerves that he could not sleep the night previous to his preaching.

But from the moment he commenced, his words, like those of a Chrysostom, enchained the attention of his hearers. His diction was so pleasing, and his language so rich, that letters of gold would not enhance their beauty. A distinguished Protestant lawyer declared he could listen to the music of Father Riordan's words when all the fashionable vagaries of the choir had ceased to interest him. As a profound mathematician, if he had an equal, he assuredly had no superior in the State. Differential calculus, and abstruse problems in geometry seemed to afford him more than ordinary recreation. When teaching and instructing, he was affable and gentle as a child; while in denouncing hypocrisy or knavery, he was confessedly sarcastic and uncompromising.

With those who have shaped the faith and patriotism of their race—the old Irishwomen —Father Riordan was an especial favorite. On the eve of all great Festivals, especially during the weeks preceding Christmas and Easter, they flocked to him from all parts of the city and surrounding country, for the purpose of "confessing" in Irish. In the course of his recreative walks, he was often detained in his pleasure to return the salute that proceeded from some silver-crowned head, nestled in bordered cap and green ribbons. To those who did not understand the language (and they were legion), their meeting and mutual felicitations would authorize the belief that a long absent child had just returned to re-visit the home of his grandparents.

His remains are interred within the inner circle of the Priests' mound in Calvary Cemetery. If avoirdupois or cubic measure betokens a generous and great heart, then, I verily believe, the biggest and best heart of all was enshrined within Father Martin Riordan's breast. He was nature's nobleman from his boots to his biretta. Although it may appear out of place, I cannot refrain from interpolating th verse from Marc Anthony's panegyric of Cæsar in so far as I consider it applicable to the life of Father Riordan.

"He was the noblest Roman of them all;
His life was gentle, and the elements so mixed in him, that nature might stand up
And say to all the world : this was a man."

On the marble slab placed over the head of his grave are inscribed these words—"*In ascensu Altaris sancti, gloriam dedit sanctitatis amictum.*"—"When he went up to the holy altar he honored the vesture of holiness."

### REV. MARTIN WALSH.

If Father Martin Walsh did not possess the superior talents and extraordinary ability, his genial qualities and priestly virtues were not second to those that adorned the life of his friend and cherished co-laborer, Very Rev. M. Riordan. I do not consider it an unguarded assertion to state that Rev. Martin Walsh had more friends than any man or woman that ever set foot in Memphis. His manly and dignified walk, as elastic as if he had just stepped out from his native Roscrea or the rock of Cashel, electrified his countrymen as he passed their doors. Defiant or boisterous Irishmen, whom a score of policemen could not disperse, would take to sudden flight at the first wave of his blackthorn. At Fairs and Pic-Nics, (when such gatherings were permitted to aid the church) Father Walsh was the man of the people. Every church device he sanctioned was sure to be a grand success. Father Walsh, with hop, skip and jump, would leave a pattern which all might imitate, but few, if any, could equal. His sonorous peal of laughter, the bright and merry twinkle of his eye often opened a miser's heart and set risible wrinkles on many a melancholy face. Having resided in the same house with this Priest for seven years, I do not hesitate to say, I never knew a more hospitable man. Every instance of past recollection leads me to believe that he never allowed a beggar or a needy person to leave his door empty-handed. His manner of relief, whether from principle or inherited example, was singularly generous, in so far that he never offered less than a dollar to any indigent applicant. Whenever the Mayor of Memphis could not assist the poor (and this was often the case), the parties were invariably directed to Father Walsh. I trust I will not incite ungenerous feelings when I express my candid belief that more blessings of the poor have been pronounced in Father Walsh's parlor and waiting-room than in any other parsonage of the diocese of Tennessee—perhaps I might include the entire district south of Mason and Dixon's line. His house was an ever open rendezvous for all city and travelling Priests. In his mirth and social intercourse he never forgot his priestly dignity. His sermons and Sunday exhortations, if they did not always bring tears, melted the pure love of God into the hearts of hearers.

Father Walsh was born in Bourna, near Roscrea, County Tipperary, Ireland. After a preparatory classical course at Nenagh (to which place he used to travel daily by the famous Bianconi coach) he became affiliated to the Archdiocese of St. Louis. He completed his theological course at St. Vincent's College, Cape Girardeau, Mo., where he received Holy Orders from the hands of the venerable Archbishop Peter Kendrick. After the consecration of Right Rev. P. A. Feehan, in '65, he left the Archdiocese to become a subject of the new diocese of Nashville. When the Fever of '78 developed, he was then obliged to use crutches, having broken his foot by a severe fall from his horse. In this pitiable condition he might be seen limping from house to house, night and day, till he contracted the Fever. He lay sick about four days, when on the 29th of August death came to his relief. He was then but forty years of age, and had heretofore enjoyed excellent health. Only three persons besides the undertaker attended his burial. Had this Priest died at any other time his funeral procession would probably reach from the city limits to the cemetery. His remains are now resting at the feet of his old friend, Very Rev. M. Riordan, and beside his cousin, Father Meagher, in Calvary Cemetery. These words are engraved on his tombstone—"*Obiit ut vixit.*"—"He died as he lived."

The Bishop of Nashville lost two other cherished friends by the Fever. When I say "cherished friends" I do not mean favorites.

At least, while he lived in Tennessee, there was no such word in the lexicon of Bishop P. A. Feehan's Administration. You might as well cavil at a man for admiring refined gold, as taunt him for loving and admiring such ingenuous Soggarths as Revs. E. Doyle and P. M. McNamara.

### REV. PATRICK McNAMARA.

This young Priest happened to be on the street when the scanty funeral of his old comrade, Father M. Walsh, passed by. He turned around and looked sadly after it. He went back to his room and never left till he was taken out a corpse. He was a native of Listowel, Co. Kerry, Ireland, and but 28 years of age at the time of his death. Being too young to receive Holy Orders when he had finished his course in All-Hallows, he went to St. Sulpice College, Paris, where he reviewed his studies while awaiting the time specified for ordination. He said his first Mass on Trinity Sunday, '73, and arrived in Nashville in September of the same year. A friend who knew him in Ireland informed me he was the youngest child of a family of twelve. All his salary and other perquisites he devoted to the purchase of a library. Accordingly at his death, if he had not the largest, he unquestionably owned the most select library in the State. Some time before the Fever of '78 he gave a course of lectures in St. Patrick's church. I have these yet in my possession. Feeling myself incapable of criticising the writings of such a profound scholar, I simply state the fact that those lectures gave more general satisfaction to the Catholics and Protestants of Memphis than the many that had previously been delivered in Memphis. When the telegram announcing his death was handed to the Bishop he simply ejaculated: "A light has been put out." Had he lived to develop his talents and the education which he received his name and fame would extend far beyond the limits of Tennessee. His veins appeared to be surcharged with the quickest blood, while his broad naked forehead bespoke reserved force and latent ability. Besides a brilliant head, "Mack," (as we familiarly called him,) had as true and generous a heart as ever throbbed within an Irish breast. Had I not been forbidden by a Priest who was then my host and superior, I would have responded to his last telegram begging me to come and see him before he died, even though I had to defy "quarantine" and risk my life. I never loved a brother as I loved this Priest. Those of his books that I still retain, I would not exchange or part with for any consideration. When each succeeding Christmas comes round, I could wish, with his fond sister Maggie, that he had enjoyed many *happy* returns of *that day.* He died two weeks before the pastor, Very Rev. M. Riordan, 4th September, 1878. He had the greatest esteem for Shakspeare. While elated by some grand idea that struck him when preparing his lectures, he would suddenly stand upon the floor of his room and in his bass, eloquent voice, declaim some passage from Shakspeare's Hamlet—

"To die—to sleep
No more; and by a sleep to say we end
The heart-aches and the thousand natural shocks
That flesh is heir to ;—'tis a consummation
Devoutly to be wished."

When I heard poor Mack declaim these lines, the last time, I little dreamt that he was so soon "to die—to sleep no more." His epitaph bears these words: "*Vixit ut dixit.*" "He lived as he said."

The mortality reported for the day on which he died exceeded two hundred.

### REV. EDWARD DOYLE.

This Priest was a native of County Carlow. He made his preparatory studies in Carlow Seminary, and his theological course in All-Hallows College, Drumcondra. He was ordained for the diocese of Nashville, where, as Priest, he remained until his death, August 4, 1879. (His assistant, Father John Fahey, died two days after, on the 6th.) Father Doyle was but 46 years old at the time of his death. In every sense he was a model Priest, and a worthy and most efficient man. In jocular parlance, the Priests used to say that unless Father Doyle died of his own accord, death could never take him, for he appeared to be as cool-tempered and cold as the grim messenger himself. Indeed, his skeleton frame seemed to be Fever proof. Although of a reticent disposition, he possessed a fund of wit and didactic knowledge. Notwithstanding he was never heard to laugh outright himself, yet by a dry stroke of wit, he could set a whole company in roars of laughter.

The death of this Priest struck me singularly, and upset a quondam theory that natural fear had a great deal to do with the death or distemper of the patient. The coolness of this man's entire life was so unalterable, I could believe that if a skeleton arose out of its grave, and flitted before him with gnashing teeth and empty sockets. E. Doyle, or, as he was sometimes styled, "Doctor" Doyle, would scarcely lift up his head to notice it. Dickens depicted no living character removed so far away from the promptings of flesh and blood as this Priest. After Vicar General M. Riordan died, in '78, the Bishop deputed Father Doyle (then pastor at Jackson) to take his place. Without a word of inquiry or a moment's delay, he at once started for St. Patrick's church, Memphis. As Father Riordan and his assistant, Father McNamara, had just died in the parsonage, Father William Walsh requested him not to remain in the city, but to accompany himself to Camp Father Mathew. He refused to comply. So long as he was enabled to attend to the spiritual wants of his people, I am convinced he would not cross the street to save himself. I do not mean to insinuate he was reckless in the exposure of his life. He was too unruffled for anything like that. He simply cared not a whit for the comforts a prolonged life could afford. He regarded it his duty to remain where the people could easily reach him. No wonder the Bishop loved this true and saintly man.

Although, in the order of seniority, he was entitled to a parish long before he was appointed pastor, still, the Bishop, knowing his usefulness and integrity, retained him at the Cathedral as secretary for more than seven years. Several months before he died, this good Priest assured me he needed not only the comforts, but some of the important necessaries of life. His retiring disposition forbade him disclose his wants. Some of his neighboring parishioners luckily discovered his destitute condition, and generously sent him a supply of coal, flour, meat, and other provisions. Some one may ask how I came to know this fact. Having already premised that the Rev. gentleman assured me himself. I now state, as his successor at St. Patrick's, that I was obliged to pay several grocery, drug, and dry goods bills, which Father Doyle's contracted finances incapacitated him to liquidate. After his death, a few pennies, and a bunch of keys, which in truth unlocked nothing precious, remained the inventory of his earthly possessions.

It will be a summary of his life to state that he had not only the sympathy and esteem of the Bishop, but he was a cherished friend of every man, woman and child that ever regarded his honest, upright face. Those who knew him in his native county, where his friends are numerous and most respectable, as also those who studied with him at All-Hallows, will bear me out in this assertion. " *Lux orta est justo,*"—" Light has arisen for the just "—is the motto over his grave. After his death, in '79, I felt honored that Bishop Feehan should appoint me to succeed him as Pastor of St. Patrick's church. Although my assistant prevailed on me to burn the bed on which the two previous Assistants, McNamara and Fahey, died, I loved to sleep on that same bed on which the venerable Father Riordan, in '78, and Father Doyle, in '79, slept and died.

### REV. J. J. MOONEY.

Rev. J. J. Mooney was a native of the city of Dublin, and was ordained for that Archdiocese. After several years' faithful and efficient service in his native city, he chose a foreign mission and emigrated to this country. He was immediately adopted by the Bishop of Nashville, in whose diocese he remained until his death, September 27, 1878. Besides performing the duties of Chaplain he taught classics and other classes for several years, in the Christian Brothers' College, Memphis. Before the Fever appeared in '78, the Bishop had just recalled him from Memphis to the Cathedral of Nashville. When he heard of so many of his brother clergymen falling victims to the plague, he considered it providential that he was so seasonably removed. Fearing the city would soon be left without a Priest, the Bishop reluctantly ordered him back again to Memphis. This Priest was so certain of his death, that before leaving Nashville he wrote his *will* and disposed of his library, ordering a certain number of Masses to be said for his soul. In a letter to a friend he deposed that he breathed the odor of Fever five miles outside Memphis. After contracting the disease he was taken to an isolated part of Camp Father Mathew, where he lived but three days.

Father James J. Mooney was a straightforward and zealous Priest. His retiring and reticent disposition won for him the respect of the students over whom he was placed, and the esteem of the clergy of the diocese. His modest demeanor, practical piety, and cheerful politeness were not affected or superficial, but natural. He was a genuine embodiment of the Irish gentleman. The piercing glare of his spectacled eyes, his genteel bow and hearty salute when meeting a Priest or trusty companion : "My Son, I'm delighted to see you," were really fascinating. He had all the animation and earnestness of a Frenchman, not only in the pulpit but in ordinary conversation. I never heard, in the drawing-room or stage, any one to equal him in the faithful rendition of an Irish song or ditty. When singing, he virtually transported himself back to his native hills, whilst the patriotism that was burning in his soul lighted up his countenance, causing the listeners to sigh for the ancient Bards and Ballads of

Ireland. He had a thorough knowledge of the Irish language. I often regretted that my most communicative language was English, when hearing Father Mooney and Vicar General Riordan exchange their "*Cead millia faltas" with that enthusiastic relish which only Gaelic patriots could enjoy. He was out-spoken in his denunciations of British misrule, and was ever ready to give full vent to his political aspirations—"that the Irish people had an indefeasible right to govern and make laws for their own country." Amongst those whom he considered a withered branch of obsolete feudalism was the entire body of English Lords, while he believed that the poorest cabin in his native country sheltered a more useful *woman* and a better family than the royal house of Hanover. I verily believe this clergyman, who had an important position in the city of Dublin, and whose family were quite affluent, would have never left Ireland if it were not for his avowed disgust of British Constabulary, Soldiery, and estated Shylocks. Of all the Priests that were sent to Nashville, I believe Father Mooney was the only one who did not wish to go to Memphis. His obedience to the order of the Bishop, on this account, deserves especial commendation.

* A hundred thousand welcomes. See G. Griffin's poem, "The Invasion."

After the manner of our Blessed Lord, he faced death—"Not my will but thine be done." *Bis emori est alterius arbitrio mori."* (Syrus.) "To die at the command of another is to die twice." He was about forty-six years of age at the time of his death. His epitaph, "*Missus ut coronatur,*"—"He was sent to be crowned," —is most befitting.

### FATHER JOHN FAHEY.

When the Fever of '78 had ceased, the surviving Priests of the city, and others, went out to see the newly-made graves of their departed brethren. As all stood around the unbroken semi-circle of graves, admiring the magnificent marble monument in the centre, Father Fahey, nudging Father Doyle, who stood beside him, in a jocular mood remarked,— "Doctor, *there* is your place next year, and *here* is mine," pointing to a blooming rose-bush that lay at his feet. Poor Father Doyle, to whom the world appeared of little consequence, sniffed a little at this selfish selection. These two Priests were the first to die the following year. Father Doyle died on the 4th, and his assistant, Father Fahey, on the 6th of August. Their bodies lay side by side, while the rose-bush blooms between them. Father Fahey was but 29 years old when he died. In addition to a handsome, pleasing face, he had a large, robust frame, capable of defying the rigors of any climate; while withal he was a man of culture and marked ability. Throughout his arduous missions, and in every city where he was stationed, he won the esteem and affection of the people.

He was born at the foot of Slievenamon, near Clonmel, County Tipperary, Ireland, and finished his studies in All-Hallows College. His tombstone bears this motto: "*Recto corde letitia.*" "Joy with a right heart."

REVS. J. A. BOKEL, O. P., J. R. McGARVEY, O. P., D. E. REVILLE, O. P., AND OTHERS.

Of the *Religious* Priests who died of Fever, I regret to state that want of personal acquaintance renders it impossible for me to furnish any interesting facts regarding their lives.

Father J. A. Bokel, O. P., who died in '78, and whose uncle was pastor of St. Peter's at the time, was but recently ordained when he was called to give up his young life for the parishioners of St. Peter's. He was but 29 years at his death.

Father McGarvey was a co-assistant with Father Bokel at St. Peter's. This young Irish-American Priest was in the prime of life and health when death overtook him, Aug. 29, '78, being then only 33 years old. He was tall and dignified. While a favorite with the older people, the little children of the parish almost idolized him. It was a pleasure to see them recognize him in the streets, and, running towards, nestle beside him until he would pat them on the head, or banter them with some extempore puzzle or pleasantry. There was an unruffled smile always on his countenance. Yellow Jack took a dreadful aim when he struck down this gifted Priest.

Rev. P. J. Scanlon, another young man of the same Order, was sent from Louisville to Memphis to fill the "gap" opened by the deaths of Fathers Bokel and McGarvey. He remained in the city but a few days when he took the Fever and died, at the age of 30.

The next year, Rev. D. E. Reville, O. P., lost his life by the Fever. This was the only son of France whose martyr-life expired in Memphis. As a pulpit orator, he was unquestionably the most eloquent in Memphis in '79. He was 39 years old.

Regarding Rev. V. B. Vantroostenberg, I regret that the want of reliable information prevents me saying further than that he was sent to Memphis, and died there in the 35th year of his age.

A similar lack of trustworthy personal history renders it impossible for me to do justice to the lives of Revs. V. G. Chrysostom Reinike, V. P. Maternus, Erasmus, and another German Franciscan, who became victims of the plague.

Although the parish attached to their Monastery in Memphis is the smallest and least lucrative, yet, as I have already insinuated, they were ever faithful in the performance of charitable deeds in aid of the sufferers during the Fever.

### REV. PATRICK RYAN.

Rev. P. Ryan was born near Nenagh, Co. Tipperary, Ireland, in the year 1840. While yet a child, he was brought to this country by his parents, who, being evicted by a ruthless landlord, were forced to emigrate. They settled in New York city, where, until his death, his mother and brothers lived. He completed his philosophic and theologic courses at St. Vincent's College, Cape Girardeau, Mo.

As I had been for two years an under classmate, I can state Father Ryan, although not possessing extraordinary talents, was one of the soundest and most reliable students of the Seminary. He knew what inexperienced collegians would not willingly acknowledge, that greater men than he lived, were living, and would live. The professors and students regarded Ryan as one whose head contained what other students had to learn from books

—*common sense.* Whenever Mr. P. Ryan was questioned in the class-room, his answers were listened to with marked deference. And yet, when out on the recreation grounds, he could find no one to equal him in hand, foot, or base ball. Indeed, few athletes could compete with him. With a bound, I often witnessed him spring over the high fence fronting the college, eliciting "three cheers" for the *Ryans* and "huzzas" for *Tipperary.*

At this time, Ryan was an enviable name. Just one year before (in '68), one of the College Faculty, Stephen V. Ryan, was raised to the Episcopate. Then there was amongst the St. Louis clerisy a silver-tongued orator of the name; while all the Southern States resounded the praises of the Poet-Priest, Rev. A. J. Ryan (R. I. P.). Many Priests of the Archdiocese of St. Louis still remember the happy days they spent at the Cape with Father P. Ryan.

He was ordained in the summer of '69, by Rt. Rev. P. A. Feehan, who sent him to Clarksville as Pastor. Soon after, Chattanooga, in the race for commercial prosperity, threatened to outstrip all the second-class cities of Tennessee. Seeing that Clarksville could never keep pace with the fast growth of its rival, the Bishop, appreciating the prudence and Priestly zeal of Father Ryan, transferred him from Clarksville to the larger field of labors in Chattanooga. Here he remained as Pastor until the Fever invaded the city, and claimed him one of its victims, in '78. His brother, Father Michael, only a few weeks ordained, was his assistant at the time. This poor man had to give his brother the last Sacraments, and was actually required to assist the undertaker while putting his body in the coffin. In the midst of the Fever of '78, Father Ryan wrote to Father William Walsh, of Memphis:

"I trust in God I shall hear better news from you. My prayers, if they can avail anything, are for your safety. May God in His great mercy give you strength and courage to bear up against this great calamity. As I cannot live without ye, I will go and die with ye. P. RYAN."

These were probably his last written words. They are a grand recommendation before God and Angels.

His remains were deposited under the shadow of his church, where they lay until Nov. 10, 1886, when they were taken from their temporary repository and re-interred in the presence of three thousand citizens in the new Catholic Cemetery, recently purchased by the present zealous Pastor, Rev. P. J. Gleason.*

* This cool-headed Priest is about to erect a new church in Chattanooga that will out-rival all the churches of the State, even the Cathedral. I trust that, when complete, Rome will invest him with a bejewelled ring, and that, since he has not died of *Yellow* Fever like his predecessor, he may *depart* in *Purple*.

# The Catholic Sisterhood in Memphis.*

Having with all the enthusiasm of a surviving comrade placed before the reader a synopsis of the lives of those self-sacrificing clergymen who fell victims to the plague while endeavoring to save the Lord's vineyard; and having, from the limited resources afforded me, employed my best endeavors to unravel all doubts that might have existed prejudicial to the godly zeal and heroic actions of those Priests who were exposed, but survived the Fever; having also striven to render impartial justice to those brave men and women of the laity who escaped the contagion; while I would have them singled out worthy not only the gratitude of Memphians but the recognition of every true christian citizen of the United States, I would consider it a serious *injustice* to overlook the virtues and valorous deeds of another band of Catholic warriors, whose unbiassed charity and untiring labors justly entitled them to be re-

---

* Of some fifty nuns who died of Yellow Fever in Memphis, I regret to state the following are all the names I could obtain:—Mother Gertrude, Sister Alphonso, Sister Rose, Sister Josepha, Sister Mary Bernardine, Sister Mary Dolora, Sister Mary Veronica, Sister Wilhelmina, Sister Vincent, Sister Stanislaus, Sister Gertrude, Sister Winkelman, Sister Frances, Sister Catherine, Sister Regina.

garded the "*right wing*" of the christian army. I make reference to the Catholic Sisterhood—the nuns of the various "Orders" that lived or died in Memphis during the epidemics of '73, '78 and '79. It is with sincere regret I have to acknowledge that all I can say in their favor in the present chapter will not requite a fraction of the praise they justly merited. I should glory in the man who would take up his gifted pen and inscribe their names in the golden pages of history. Those "*Doves* of the *temple*" have merited the benisons of the poor and suffering of every creed and nationality. If the discharge of duty demanded the sacrifice of twenty-three Priests, the Sisterhood had a death-roll of at least fifty. Like the majority of the Priests, those of them who died were in the bloom of youth and health, naturally expecting to spend the summer and survive a portion of the winter of human life, serving God and doing good amongst men, according to the dictates of their precious "calling."

In the world, the parent is thoroughly satisfied, if not frequently overjoyed when the young daughter returns to her home a *graduate* from the High School or Seminary. But amongst the "*departed*" were young women of refined education and intellect not merely graduates in philology, music and other fine arts, but christian ladies who had attained a *graduateship* in the schools of humility, chastity and religion. Their mission is entirely shut out from the world in times of peace and prosperity. But no sooner does the bugle of war resound, or the foul breath of pestilence diffuse its poisonous influence, than the rusty locks and iron bolts of the convent gate are driven back. Now the world and those who heretofore did not commune with the world, meet face to face. The hand that told the beads or clasped the Little Office Book, may now be seen chafing the fevered brow or ministering the cooling draught.

If a case of Fever had never occurred in Memphis, some of the citizens would betray either a lack of memory or gratitude should they have forgotten the kind hands that bound their wounds, staunched their blood, and wiped their bespattered and parched faces. There is still living in Memphis many a brave old soldier in broadcloth or rags, who yet retains the beads or scapular placed around his neck on the battle-field, and who can never see a Catholic Nun (whom he generally calls a Sister of Charity,) without associating her with the woebegone days of Shiloh, Gettysburg, Fort Sumter and Vicksburg.

When the female youth of America are appalled at the first announcement of Small-pox or Cholera, from out the convent gate you see a little regiment of black or white-robed Sisters marching to those localities that are poorest and most afflicted. Their gentle "tap" is heard a thousand times oftener at the door of the needy, than at the electric button in the hall of the lordly mansion. When peace and order have been restored, the cloister gates are again locked to all except the youth whom they would enroll imitators of Jesus and Children of Mary. They teach them the *principles* of christian perfection, while they instill into their young hearts traits of philanthropy and true womanhood—*blessings* of more value to them here and hereafter than real estate deeds or miserable pelf. Each of the five female religious "Orders"[*] that lived in Memphis during the past twenty years have conferred untold blessings on the city and citizens of Memphis. Bending over the pallet of some wretched beggar or ruined creditor, they point to him a "home" beyond the stars and remind him of a God who shall requite their losses and end their sufferings. The child whose parents death snatched to a premature grave no longer appears a homeless waif as he nestles beside the Superioress or Sisters of the convent. The abandoned outcast, whom no respectable man or woman

---

[*] Orders:—Dominican, Franciscan, Good Shepherd, Josephite, and Charity.

would salute, finds a home with those ministering "Angels." Instead of jocund curses and jeers, to which their ears were accustomed, they exhort them to join in hymns and prayers to Jesus and Mary Immaculate.

The natural parent may furnish the State with a well-developed soldier or citizen; a young woman of graceful form and gifted intellect; but the youthful training of the *soul* and *heart*, under the tutelage of the Sisters, has often inspired the soldier with sentiments of loyalty and courage, who otherwise would be a traitor; saved the law-abiding citizen, who would be a wayward prodigal; and made the young woman a God-fearing, virtuous ornament, instead of a frivolous devotee of vanity or dissipation.

In view of all these services, it is discouraging to think that they sometimes are allowed to suffer. When teachers and nurses in the world receive most flattering recompense for their services, the Sisters are often allowed to come and go without receiving any visible recognition for their labors. After the Fever of '79, I remember standing over the graves of those fifty martyr-heroines, and although I knew that both in life and death they cared not for worldly pomp or display, still, I felt sorry for the surviving populace who could bear to look without remorse on those "mounds" devoid of wooden or marble slab.†

## THE SISTER OF CHARITY.

#### GERALD GRIFFIN.

She once was a lady of honor and wealth,
Bright glow'd on her features the roses of health;
Her vesture was blended of silk and of gold,
And her motion shook perfume from every fold.
Joy revelled around her—love shone at her side,
And gay was her smile as the glance of a bride;
And light was her step in the mirth-sounding hall,
When she heard of the daughters of Vincent de Paul.

She felt in her spirit the summons of grace,
That call'd her to live for the suffering race;
And, heedless of pleasure, of comfort, of home,
Rose quickly, like Mary, and answered, "I come."
She put from her person the trappings of pride,
And pass'd from her home with the joy of a bride,
Nor wept at the threshold, as onward she moved,
For her heart was on fire in the cause it approved.

Lost ever to fashion—to vanity lost—
That beauty that once was the song and the toast;
No more in the ball-room, that figure we meet,
But gliding at dusk to the wretch's retreat.
Forgot in the halls, is that high-sounding name,
For the Sister of Charity blushes at fame;
Forgot are the claims of her riches and birth,
For she barters for heaven the glory of earth.

---

† The few Episcopal Sisters who fell were all but immortalized by the members of their church. The Relief Bureau of Hartford, Connecticut, sent the following:

"*Resolved*, that we offer this loving tribute in memory of Sister Constance, to her late associates, to the Mother Superior of her Order, to her Pastor, Rev. Dr. Harris, and to Right Rev. Dr. Quintard, (Protestant) Bishop of Tennessee, with our heartfelt sympathy and prayers.

MRS. F. E. HARDIMAN, Pres.
MRS. JNO. BROCKLESBY, Vice-Pres.
MRS. SARAH E. DAVIS, Rec. Secr'y.

Hartford, Conn., Oct. 4, 1878."

## THE SISTER OF CHARITY.

Those feet that to music could gracefully move,
Now bear her alone on the mission of love;
Those hands that once dangled the perfume and gem,
Are tending the helpless or lifted for them;
That voice that once echo'd the song of the vain,
Now whispers relief to the bosom of pain;
And the hair that was shining with diamond and pearl,
Is wet with the tears of the penitent girl.

Her down-bed—a pallet, her trinket—a bead,
Her lustre—one taper that serves her to read;
Her sculpture—the crucifix nail'd by her bed,
Her paintings—one print of the thorn-crowned head;
Her cushion—the pavement that wearies her knees,
Her music—the psalm, or the sigh of disease.
The delicate lady lives mortified there,
And the feast is forsaken for fasting and prayer.

Yet not to the service of heart and of mind,
Are the cares of that heaven-minded virgin confined;
Like him whom she loves, to the mansions of grief,
She hastes with the tidings of joy and relief.
She strengthens the weary, she comforts the weak,
And soft is her voice in the ear of the sick;
Where want and affliction on mortals attend,
The Sister of Charity, there is a friend.

Unshrinking where pestilence scatters his breath,
Like an Angel she moves 'mid the vapor of death;
Where rings the loud music and flashes the sword,
Unfearing she walks, for she follows the Lord.
How sweetly she bends o'er each plague-tainted face,
With looks that are lighted with holiest grace;
How kindly she dresses each suffering limb,
For she sees in the wounded the image of Him.

Behold her, ye worldly! Behold her, ye vain!
Who shrink from the pathway of virtue and pain;
Who yield up to pleasure your nights and your days,
Forgetful of service, forgetful of praise.
Ye lazy philosophers,—self-seeking men,—
Ye fireside philanthropists,—great at the pen,—
How stands in the balance your eloquence weighed,
With the life and the deeds of that high-born maid?

## THE FEVER-PROOF LITTLE BAND OF ST. JOSEPH HEROINES.*

During all the plagues that visited Memphis, including '73, '78 and '79, there was a little band (six St. Joseph Sisters) that seemed to be Fever-proof. After the financial depression of '78 had discouraged all prospects for their academy, the Mother Superioress in St. Louis (Agatha) required them to give up their Memphis Mission. This happened a little before the Fever broke out in '79. There was a suppressed rumor that they left in anticipation of the Fever. To frustrate this unfounded report, I applied to the Mother Superioress, acquainting her of the inopportuneness of the departure of the Sisters. She told me that, if Bishop Ryan consented, she would gladly send them back. I applied to the Bishop, who had no objection. I returned to Carondelet to acquaint the Mother. I naturally supposed there would be considerable reluctance on the part of those who were to be sent to Memphis—then regarded everywhere as a certain grave-depot. Would you believe? Double the number requisite cheerfully volunteered. I trust it is not a revelation of convent secrecy when I state that one little sister called me aside, and begged me to

*Mother Leone; Sisters Immaculate, Antoinette, Irene, Clarissa and De Sales.

ask the Mother to let her go to Memphis.

Few ladies of the world could go to a ball or marriage feast with more breathless enthusiasm than these saintly creatures went to face death. On their way to Memphis, the six chosen ones were stopped at Humboldt (82 miles from Memphis), on account of quarantine regulations. They were sadly discouraged seeing that their journey was impeded. A generous Lady of Humboldt, Mrs. Donovan, entertained them until Bishop Feehan obtained permission for them to proceed. They went directly to Camp Father Mathew, where they spent their nights. Every morning they walked to the city, carrying large baskets filled with provisions, money and medicine, for the sick and poor. They were now in, and again out of, the Camp. In the little band was a deaf Sister called A——. She is at present an enfeebled invalid in Douglas Asylum, Chicago. Men of every persuasion regarded her as a veritable Saint. She consoled broken-hearted widows; fed and sheltered abandoned orphans; she not only sat with the sick and dying, but saw they were decently shrouded, encoffined, and buried. There is no record or history of this little Sister's heroism; yet she had bravery enough to honor her entire sex. I trust it will not, (if she still lives) wound her virgin humility to say that her smiling face, and her kind consoling words have melted into the hearts of many a bereaved husband, disconsolate widow, and orphan waif, the love and charity of Jesus Christ. The poor negro, who until '78 never took, and was never supposed to take the Fever, often blessed her name as he took the refreshing draught from her white and wasted hands. It is singular, if not remarkable, that while every "Order" of Nuns and Priesthood in Memphis was decimated by the plague, not a single one of St. Joseph's Sisters died or took the fever. If it is not ludicrous, I can offer no other explanation of their escape—they imbibed an *overdose* of "sporadic infection." Unless we have recourse to the supernatural, there is no other way to unravel this mystery. It is not saying too much—this Sister A—— has seen more Yellow Fever patients than any human individual, male or female, in North or South America.

> " Softly and noiselessly some feet tread
>   Lone ways on earth without leaving a mark ;
> They move 'mid the living, they pass to the dead
>   As still as the gleam of a star thro' the dark.
>     Sweet lives those
>     In their strange repose "
>             —*Father Ryan.*

## INCIDENTS OF THE FEVER OF 1878.

The reader will bear in mind that out of a population of more than fifty thousand, thirty thousand had fled the city before the 18th of August; 19,600 remained either through necessity or the greedy hope of enriching themselves during this extraordinary crisis. Eight hundred citizens took refuge in camp Williams (five miles from Memphis), and four hundred in Camp Father Mathew (four miles from Memphis). Of those who remained in the city 14,000 were colored, leaving only 6,000 white people; 946 colored and 4,204 whites died in the city during the autumn. Not more than two hundred whites escaped the Fever, and most of these had been victims of it in previous years.

Amongst the run-aways were several prominent city officials, several physicians, and almost all the Preachers of the town. It would not be correct to say all left. Doctors Harris and White, and Rev. C. Parsons of the Episcopal Church, Dr. Boggs and Rev. Landrum of the Presbyterian, and Rev. E. C. Slater of the Methodist church, remained in the city. The Ministers who died of Fever were: Rev. Mr. Parsons, Rev. E. C. Slater, Rev. P. T. Scruggs, and Rev. Mr. Thomas (German Reformed). Some three or four volunteer

Ministers also died, but as they had no special charge in Memphis at the time, I do not think it fair to rank them with the Memphis Ministers.

When the Fever broke out in '78, there were in Memphis five Catholic and fifty-three Protestant churches; of the latter, twenty-four were white and twenty-nine colored. The white congregations were as follows:— three Baptist; one Christian; one Congregational; two Cumberland Presbyterian; four Episcopal; one Lutheran; one Israelite; six Methodist and five Presbyterian. When the Fever broke out in '78, there were in Memphis eleven Priests; twelve died during the epidemic, and three survived. It may be considered unfair that I do not accredit the Protestant church with the four volunteers who died of the Fever, while I compute the Priests sent to Memphis as adding lustre to its martyr record. I do not mean to do injustice to any religious sect. The volunteer Preachers who came to Memphis or died there, differ from the Priests who were *sent*, in the fact that the former had no *local* charge. A Priest wishing to go to a plague-stricken city, depends on the Bishop for "*faculties*." The "*willingness*" of a clergyman" in the Catholic church does not presuppose his approval. Were I to reckon the volunteer Ministers who succumbed, as adding to their local mortality list, I should, for a similar reason, include three Catholic Priests who went to die in Memphis during the Fever; but who were not approved by the Bishop of the diocese.

In page 124 of Mr. J. M. Keating's History of Yellow Fever, he says:—"A few ill-conditioned zealots, taking advantage of this state of the public mind, made comparisons between the Protestant Ministers and the Catholic Priests, which the circumstances did not warrant, with a view to injure the Protestant churches. But this failed." Very good. I trust it did fail. But let us see if we can reconcile Hon. J. M. Keating the *Author* of the Yellow Fever History, with Hon. J. M. Keating, the illustrious *Editor* of the *Memphis Appeal*, to whom I never atttributed a dual existence.

Referring to the Protestant Ministers, the *Memphis Appeal* of 1878 gave the following scathing rebuke to those who deserted their flocks:

"They left their communities to die like dogs, without one word of consolation or hope. * * * They left no excuse that a suffering people can bear to hear. * * * They have strengthened the mother church, against whom it was their habit to inveigh as the 'scarlet woman.' * * * They have literally denied their Lord and Master. 'I was sick and ye visited me not.' * * * Their bad example has become contagious, as witness Chattanooga, where only two ministers remained, and both of them, God help them, in their death-beds."

This, Hon. J. M. Keating, is a fearful invective, which appears to me, if not undeserved, unquestionably too sarcastic. "They left their communities to *die* like *dogs.*" It is too severe. What could those ministers do in case they remained? They had no *necessary* Sacraments they could administer at the hour of death. They could only visit or nurse the sick. But is a minister, with or without a wife and family, obliged to risk human life for the sake of merely visiting or nursing a member of his flock? The city supplied plenty of nurses. Before or after an epidemic a Protestant minister is not bound, *ex-officio*, to visit all his patients, or even to give all members funeral rites. These are generally solemnized in quiet times. But I deny, according to Protestant tenets, that a soul is endangered by their non-fulfillment. A Minister, then, who neglects to visit a sick member, or fails to perform "funeral rites," is not to be regarded as letting him "die like a *dog.*" Even in the Catholic church, "*funeral service*" is not of necessity. But a Priest has no plea, like a Minister, to abandon his flock. Each member regards him as a spiritual Father. His presence is required to regenerate him in baptism, forgive him his sins, nourish him during life, and, when death comes, to be there, to hand him over to his

Creator. If the reception of the Sacraments is necessary during life, Catholic faith teaches they are indispensable (extremely necessary) at the hour of death. The Minister can say at any time, "I can do no more for this member of my flock." The Priest can never say this while there is a living breath in the good or ungodly. Unfortunately, many Catholics defer half a century of repentance till the moment of death. Even though there are no very bright promises in his favor, still it would be rendering the Redeeming Merits of our Lord nugatory, were the Priest to absent himself in such a crisis. "I will not the death of a sinner, but rather, that he be converted and live." There is a christian "leave-taking" between the Priest and penitent at the hour of death.

The Protestant Ministers who remained in Memphis during the epidemic may be credited for philanthropy and christian charity, but I am not disposed to insinuate those who ran away incurred any special opprobrium. All honor is due to those of them who fell victims. Still, I think the Ministers who, after the Fever had passed, came back with their smiling wives and laughing little boys and girls, did nothing so very cruel to humanity or their respective flocks. I think we might reconcile their case with the adage: "A live

*Corporal* is better than a dead *Emperor.*" The *Memphis Appeal,* which, indeed, is one of the leading papers in the South, followed up the Ministers in '78 pretty severely. In one of its articles, it wrote of Dr. Graves, the editor of the Memphis *Southern Baptist.* [I would state this Graves, every inch a bigot, often gave the Nuns, Priests, and sometimes the Pope himself, an unmerciful scathing.] The *Appeal* goes on to relate that this Dr. Graves left Memphis for California, where he was to lecture (and likely to give the Pope another scratch). On reaching Salt Lake City, he became prostrated with Yellow Fever. He was taken in charge and nursed to convalescence by the Catholic Sisters of that city. "Rather strange coincidence," comments the *Appeal.* "The leader of the Baptists of the South stricken down in a Mormon city, and receiving the christian charities and attentions of the Catholic Sisters."

To a stranger the aspect of Memphis during the epidemic was most appalling. The principal thoroughfares as well as the lanes, alleys and side-walks, were saturated with lime, carbolic acid, and other ill-odored disinfectants. The streets were obscured with smoke of ignited tar and other evaporant combustibles, with a view to scatter or dissipate the *spores.* Bedsteads, ticks, blankets, whereupon patients died, might be seen burning at almost every street corner. You might walk or ride several miles on Main street, the principal thoroughfare, and not meet five persons. Wagons and carriages were so seldom seen that their appearance lent an air of dreariness to the scene. Although horse cars were few and far between, still much credit is due to the Superintendent, Mr. Barrett, for his perseverance in running a few cars to accommodate the public in this eventful time. To take a birds-eye view of Memphis, a person should enter one of those cars. It would seem that every composite that admitted a disgusting odor was in requisition. While some outvied their proximate neighbors in the lavish use of cologne, musk, and rose-water, others armed with onions or assafœtida, seemed to issue a challenge to the nasal organs of all the passengers, if not to the city at large. Such precautions on the part of those who sought to repel the infection of Fever by such unsavory odors, appeared to me very unwise. Common sense would dictate that anything so disgusting and nauseous must offend the stomach, which, during an epidemic should, for no cause, be disarranged. If an epidemic did not exist at all, it was ominous and dreadful to see men and women on the streets and cars having large sponges attached to their noses, while others appeared to be so reckless, that one would either suppose they had, or would expose themselves to have the Fever. Outside each undertaker's shop were piles, if not mountains, of coffins or improvised boxes for the poor. The only evidence of living humanity seemed to be the hearses and vehicles carrying the dead to the different Cemeteries. The most dreadful sense of horror was the fact that, in a short time, those ghastly sights would fail to inspire terror. You would begin to get used to all these sad and sickening sights. The howling of dogs, the piteous mewing of cats, and the lowing of cattle left behind by their owners, would almost convey an idea of the terrors of the last Judgment. In some instances I was assured that faithful dogs were found dead over their masters' or mistresses' graves, while others, having nothing to eat, scooped open some of the newly made pauper-graves. Indeed, it appeared an act of mercy to feed those famished brutes. Some of those dumb creatures deserved a better end. After the death of Father Riordan, V. G., a little canine pet never left the premises during the Fever. The colored man who took charge of the Pastor's residence, stated that little Jack would *tear* any stranger who dared enter the parsonage grounds while he was in charge. Another little pet slept in the Camp at night, and every day was sure to accompany the Priest in all his visits to the sick. Father Walsh, who died in '78, had a large Newfoundland that, on hearing the clock strike twelve, used to run out and catch in his mouth the bell-rope—an exercise in which he playfully joined the Sexton as he tolled the Angelus.

But the most pitiful and heart-rending scenes were the cries and wails of bereaved mothers, wives, children, and husbands. There is something touchingly sad in hearing a man audibly weep. The ravings of some bordered on blasphemy, as they challenged the mercy of God to give them such a *stroke*. While the sufferings of some appeared to be moderate, others endured excruciating agony. Some patients died smiling, singing, or immoderately laughing; while others felt as though their blood and entrails were boiling. A lady assured me the thirst she endured caused her more suffering than parturition, cholera and small pox, in each of which, during her married life, she suffered a world of agony. Many of those who fled the city at first, were forced to return (owing to lack of funds) before the Fever had ceased. Almost every case proved fatal. The sexton of St. Bridget's church and his cousin (as stated in page 129) remained away from Memphis till

late in November, when frost had appeared.
At this time quarantine was removed, and
the city was said to be perfectly safe. Yet
those two young men were scarcely home a
week when they took the Fever and died
(Nov. 21st). Frost certainly destroys Fever,
but in order to be effective, it must be a *severe
frost*. Speaking of '78, I believe that cases
occurred in the city as early as the latter
part of July, while there is no doubt but
there were isolated cases as late as Nov. 30.
The Fever of '78 was said to have been imported from \*Grenada, a small town in Mississippi, where it caused frightful havoc. I
have no grounds to deny or doubt this assumption. But how did the succeeding Fever
of '79 originate? I heartily believe the poison
was never destroyed from its first outbreak in
'78 till the latter months of '79. I believe
the infection, spore, or whatever else it is,
remained latent throughout the winter, and
only wanted sufficient heat to develop it.

---

\* Some attribute the importation of Fever to passengers who landed from the infected steam-tug, J. D. Porter; others, that friends of Squire Pat. Winters imported it from steamer "Golden Crown."

# Thrilling Incidents of the Epidemic of '78.

The following thrilling incidents of the Yellow Fever of '78 are mostly taken from the daily Memphis papers published during the epidemic:—

AVALANCHE, Sept. 5th.—" Great God! How this murderous work has increased. Those that are left are busy burying their dead; those that are left may be taken to-morrow. * * * Impotence lies at the feet of Omnipotence, and grovels there in the dust. Yesterday's record is run up, and in all its blackness lifts its death's head and defies the best plague that ever did a job of slaying among the children of men. * * * * Who has the heart to use the multiplication in the arithmetic of sorrow, and figure out the hearts broken, the lives embittered, the houses desolated ? * * * Surely our cup of sorrow must be full. Black as the dead list is, to-day, in our city, it fails to represent all those ready for burial yesterday. The county undertaker has four furniture wagons busy all day. Upon each, the coffins were piled as high as safety from falling would permit. These four great vehicles, doing the wholesale burying business, failed to take to the potters' field all of the indigent dead. At the time the officer made his report sixty bodies were awaiting interment."

AVALANCHE, Sept. 1st.—" The king of terrors continues to snatch victims with fearful rapidity. * * * But three short weeks ago our city was active with business of all classes; our people were happy and prosperous. * * * Now, our streets are deserted, our stores and residences empty, and out of a population of more than fifty thousand, barely five thousand remain, and of those, nearly five hundred are in the grave, and perhaps double that number lie suffering with racking pains and burning fevers.

The dead body of a negro woman was found at No. 13 Commerce street, Sept. 3, her living babe trying to nurse from her putrid breast.

Visitor Anderson, of the Howards, Sept. 4th, found J. Rivière in a dying condition at No. 81 Main street. He was alone, stark naked and covered with flies.

Sept. 5th.—Annie Cook, the keeper of a bagnio on Gayoso street, who had most heroically devoted herself to the care of the sick since the fever set in, was down with a bad case of fever, from which she died two days later. (*Keating's History.*) Mr. Keating says: "This woman's faith has made her whole, and she is now in peace." In reply, I can furnish no better argument than that given in page 125 of Mr. Keating's own book:— "The ignorance of the dark ages still hangs in gloomy folds about us. Can five minutes' religious services over a poor fellow-(woman) covered with blisters, choked with black vomit, and barely able to tell his (her) nurse what he (she) wants, probably not that, renovate a moral nature, steeped in unbelief and sin for fifty years, blanch the blackness of a purely wicked life to snowy whiteness, and fit for angelic associates a man (woman) who, if he (she) ever recover would laugh at the idea of wishing religious services at the time his (her) death was deemed at hand?" (D. A. Q.)

"The sexton of St. Patrick's church reported a case where a man was shrouded and encoffined, but who, when the lid was about to be screwed down, opened his eyes and asked those performing the last offices for him. "What are you doing?" A little trepidated, if not consternated, they lifted him from his close confinement and put him to bed. After judicious treatment, he recovered." (*Keating's History.*)

[The sexton of St. Patrick's, Mr. Pat. O'Rourke, assured me this was a falsehood, as far as he was concerned.—D. A. Q.]

Sept. 14.—The Flack family were entirely annihilated. The mother, four daughters and two sons all died in one week.

APPEAL, Oct. 5th.—"On Sunday last, a number of heart-stricken citizens repaired to Elmwood Cemetery for the purpose of visiting the fresh made graves of their loved and lost, and spreading flowers on the earth hillocks that marked those sacred spots. But to their horror and dismay, the graves of the dead could not be found. This is a horrible fact to have to disclose, because it is well calculated to awaken the deepest alarm in the minds of hundreds of citizens who had their loved ones interred at Elmwood Cemetery. It will be well to remember how the dead daily encumbered the graveyard, and how hundreds of coffins lay around Elmwood daily, awaiting interment, which had to be postponed for days, owing to the scarcity of grave-diggers, or the sickness of those in charge of the cemetery during the gloomy days of September, when the Fever pest gathered in two hundred victims a day. As relatives could not wait to see their dead interred, this care often devolved on men who paid little attention to their work. On Sunday last a man had flowers to place on the grave of his wife. Although he was the owner of a private lot in the cemetery, he failed to find the coffin that contained his wife's remains. This man entertained the horrible belief that his wife was buried in a ditch or trench, in the section reserved for paupers."

Probably the most pitiable case was that of the McKinley family on Brinkley avenue, all of whom died.

Their appeal sent to the Howards was:—"For God's sake, come to us; we are all dying." The Howard visitor who was sent to them found one of the children, who had been dead three days, so far in decomposition that its abdomen had broken open, and maggots were crawling from it. Another child had been dead a day, and all of the family were sick without any attendance whatever.

Captain Rogers, who lived in Tennessee street, was nursed by two negroes sent by the Masons. When he died, some of his friends ordered the nurse to lay him out in his Masonic regalia, telling them they would find it in the wardrobe. The nurses, in their ignorance, found a grotesque suit of clothes which the poor gentleman had worn at Mardi Gras the previous year, and he was buried in them before the mistake was discovered.

Susan Cunningham, residing on Carroll avenue, had black vomit two different times in four days. Her attending physician reduced her temperature from 104° to 96°, but it went up again to 105°. It was again reduced to 97°, but went up again to 106°, from which it was again reduced to 97°; and yet she recovered.

Mr. Fred. Brennan, local editor of the *Appeal*, was in bed ten weeks, having, perhaps, the worst case of Yellow Fever on record. He had black vomit three times, and the hiccoughs twice—once for twenty-four hours, and once for eight hours—and yet he recovered. A vigorous constitution and a will that nothing could break down brought him through.

The owner of a cotton-gin, a man of wealth, sporting diamonds and fast horses, left his three sisters and an aged father without means, and subject to the fever, and fled the city. Madam Vincent was buried on Sunday, 22d September.

A kind-hearted lady was going to see a sick friend, when she heard her name called. Turning, she saw a slender girl, dressed in mourning, advancing towards her. As the child came nearer, she recognized in her the daughter of a neighbor who had died the day before, near the city. The little girl threw her arms about the lady, and sobbing, cried, "You aren't afraid of me, are you?" "No, my dear," was the soothing response. "Everybody else is," said the poor child. "They won't come near me, because papa died of the Fever, and we were with him, I and mamma." (*Keating's History.*)

Dr. Nelson, a man of considerable wealth, Thos. F. McCall, a prominent merchant, and a Mr. Kenney, a cotton planter and speculator, all died of Fever, and now sleep in unknown Potter's fields.

Said a nurse: "I came from Shreveport on Sunday, got here Monday, went to work Tuesday; Wednesday, my patient was beautiful; Thursday, he was tolerable; Thursday night, he was restless; Friday, he was dead; and Saturday, he was in hell, for all that I know. Oh, I tell you them was times, when they went to heaven and the other place by telegraph, and not over the wires either,—no, indeed!" (*Keating's History.*)

Jeff. Davis, Jr., (son of the ex-Confederate President) died at five o'clock in the evening of Oct. 16th, at Buntyn station, near Memphis.

A heavy black frost was the pleasing spectacle that gladdened the sight of the many who were on the lookout for it, on the morning of Oct. 19. This harbinger of returning health to Memphis caused unalloyed joy.—*Appeal*. [Still, cases remained as late as November 30.— D. A. Q.]

### EXTRACT FROM KEATING'S YELLOW FEVER HISTORY.

The following eloquent description of the epidemic in Memphis is taken from Keating's Yellow Fever History of '78:

"By the last week in August all who could, had fled, and all were in camp who would go. There were then about three thousand cases of Fever in the city. During its prevalence the temperature averaged from 72° to 82°. * * * An appalling gloom hung over the doomed city. At night, it was silent as the grave; by day it seemed desolate as the desert. The solemn oppressions of universal death bore upon the human mind, as if the day of Judgment were about to dawn. * * * Death prevailed everywhere; white women were seldom to be met; children, never. The voice of prayer was lifted up only at the bed of pain and death. Tears for loved ones were choked back by the feeling of uncertainty provoked by the sad condition of another. The wife was borne to the tomb while the husband was unconscious of his loss; and whole families were swept away in such quick succession that not one had knowledge of the other's departure. Death dealt kindly by these; there was no mourning; no widows; no orphans. The parents went first, in a few hours the children followed. In some instances the parents were left dazed—stunned, in a condition beyond tears and bordering on insanity. In one such case, a mother thus left, turned from her griefs with a brave heart, sustained by a holy trust, to nurse the sick. Her losses and trials deepened her sympathies and enabled her to appreciate the disheartened condition of those yet in the valley of the shadow through which she had passed. She entered the sick room with all the confidence of a martyr, dispensing the holy assurance of a saint. There was almost healing in her touch. A man, also, thus bereft, who, in one short week buried all his pets, who rose from a sick bed to lay his wife away forever, also became a nurse, and for weeks went about doing good. Others as sadly bereft, prayed for death to release them from sorrows that could not be assuaged. Sadder cases than these were the orphans, who lost both parents, children who were dropped from comfort into poverty, and robbed in a few hours of the care, protection and guidance of loving parents, to become inmates of public asylums. * * * * Some of the dead were found in a state a little better than a lot of bones in a puddle of green water. Half the putrid remains of a negro woman were found in an outbuilding near the Appeal Office, the other half had been eaten by rats that were found dead by hundreds near the spot. Many of the dead were put away in trenches, where the paupers and the unknown sleep peacefully together. The carnival of death was now at its height. Women were found dead, their little babes gasping in the throes of death, beside the breasts at which they had tugged in vain One case is recalled where the babe was literally glued to the bosom, where it had found food and shelter, and perhaps expired at the same moment as the mother. whose love was evidenced even in a death embrace. Others passed away after the labors of birth had supervened upon the fever—mother and child being buried in the same grave. The penalties of maternity, which always command the tenderest sympathy, were paid in nameless agonies, leading, in all but two cases, to forfeiture of life.

Some who had passed safely into the vigor of old age were again taxed with functions long since silenced, and in the moment of death, and even after it, this curse of the sex asserted itself to an amazing degree. Not a few were affected with swellings that took on the form of goitre, increasing the disgusting consequences of a disease, that, to the patient, is one of the most offensive — as much so as small pox, or the black plague of the East. Its effects upon men were equally forbidding. * * * Those whose physical system had received injuries which are the special penalty of lecherous excesses, died soonest. But neither cleanliness nor right living were a shield to stay the hand of this destroyer. He invaded the homes of the most chaste and the den of the vilest. He took innocence and infamy at the same moment, and spread terror everywhere. * * * There were no funerals, and but little demand for funeral service. In most cases, the driver of the hearse and his assistant comprised the funeral party. * * * *

The bell at the graveyard gate was for a long time tolled by a lovely girl who for weeks was her father's only help. She kept the registry of the dead, and knew what havoc the Fever had made. At last, sickness conquered her physical energies; but she recovered and resumed her self-selected post. No other bell save that of death was tolled. Churches were closed. Congregations were dispersed—the members were far apart—some were safe, and many were dead. The Police were cut down from forty-one to seven. The Fire Department were cut down to thirteen—their bells, too, were silenced, out of tender regard for the sick—so changed do rugged and even rough men become in the presence of an overwhelming calamity. Fortunately there were but few fires, and these made no great demands upon the energies of the Department. But petty thieving prevailed like an epidemic. A few who came to nurse, died, leaving full trunks of silverware, bric-a-brac and clothing. A few also made themselves notorious for lewdness and drunkenness. To these many deaths may be ascribed. They shocked decency and outraged humanity. They were no better than the beasts of the field. They made of the epidemic a carnival. But the worst of them were cut short in their career; only one or two escaped with their lives. One of these, a woman, while stupefied from wine and brandy, allowed a poor woman to leave her bed, naked as when born, and wander out in the country on an inclement night, calling as she went, for the husband who had preceded her to the grave by a few days. In the house of an ex-judge, whence a whole family had been borne to the grave, the victims of neglect, four such nurses died, and in the two trunks of one—and the worst of them, a woman of seeming refinement—there was found the family plate, and wearing apparel of the judge's wife, then absent in Ohio. This woman and her paramours fell victims to the Fever they invited by their debaucheries, and hastened by their excesses. In the whole range of human depravity there are few parallels to these cases. They illustrate extreme degradation; they sounded the lowest depths of vice, and shamed even the low standard of savage life. At a time when the hearts of nearly all were filled with sorrow and weighed with care, they gave way to the vilest and most brutal of human weaknesses, and surrendered themselves to shamelessness that horrified decency."

## SOME OUTSPOKEN FACTS.

It is a fact which neither religious humility should conceal, nor bigoted knavery belittle, that the Priests of the diocese of Nashville, guided by their good Bishop, have afforded a noble exemplar, not only to clergy, but have furnished a *golden chapter* for the future history of Catholicism in America.

I have stated that Very Rev. J. A. Kelly,

O. P., had survived the three plagues of '73, '78 and '79; that, although Vicar General M. Riordan had leave of absence when the Fever invaded Memphis in '78, yet, when hearing of the death of his comrades, he returned immediately to the city.

I have stated Father William Walsh, the present pastor of St. Bridget's church, left his aged parents in Ireland, and bade what he might reasonably call a *last farewell* to his native home; yet, like a *very* warrior going to another battle, he spared neither time nor expense to return to his flock.

I have elsewhere designated Father Aloysius Weiver, the unrequited, but veritable hero of Memphis. He was night and day at the service of the people. While friends were leaving friends, and brothers, brothers and sisters, this saintly father stood over the bed of the hopeless and helpless. Instead of donning a lighter and cooler garment, he chose to stalk among the lanes and thoroughfares in coarse brown habit and sandals that merely protected the soles of his feet.

Father P. Ryan, when his application to go to Memphis was not accepted, was soon to lay down his life among his own beloved people of Chattanooga. His brother, as I have stated (Father Michael), had to give him the last Sacraments, and assist in putting his corpse in the coffin. After having buried his brother, the Bishop called him to Nashville. Before entering this city, he had to invest himself with a suit of new clothes, being ordered to bury outside the suburbs the garments he wore while in Chattanooga. Soon after the epidemic had ceased, and while the odor of Fever was yet about him, he was sent to Memphis as assistant to Father Quinn, then pastor of St. Patrick's church. Although a young man of marked ability, his mind gradually gave way. At present, he is a demented inmate of St. Vincent's Hospital, St. Louis. (May God award him a martyr's crown.)

The Priests' mound in Calvary cemetery, Memphis, enshrines the bones of veritable martyrs. If these men are not such, then "dying for the *faith* and our *fellow-men*" is not martyrdom. The fact of Jesus *dying* for *men* is the most emphatic proof of incarnate love. Only some three or four Priests were bound *ex-officio* to remain in the city during the plague. All the others, without risk of reputation, could have saved their lives. They could be living now (like you, good reader), preparing for the peaceful advent of death in the midst of sympathizing friends, expecting to see "silver threads" commingle with their ebon or golden locks. No one shirked back to the rear ranks; every soldier of the church stood in the van, and defied the arrows of death. This Christian squadron was not a heedless or a headless body. It was capital, corporate, and well organized as any army, having inferior and superior officers, guided by a vigilant Captain. All, even those who were bound to remain in the city, fought like jaded disciples.

It is but trite tautology to state those Priests were neither *Gods* nor *Angels;* they were *men*, having human sympathies and domestic relations. (I have stated one was the youngest child of a family of twelve). When the wires and cables spread the tidings of their deaths, not only in this country was there wide-spread mourning, but far beyond the broad Atlantic; in Tipperary, Limerick, Cork, Kerry, Waterford, Kilkenny, Carlow, Clare, and Cavan—yes, and farther East and South-East: in Belgium, France and Germany, aged parents wept and wished that God had taken them first. Since their "departure," many a loving brother and sister have missed the long-expected and ever-welcome letter that bore the beautiful device, "The *Goddess* of *Liberty*," and conveyed sentiments of Hope, Love, and Life Eternal.

But it may be argued that death is sure to come, soon or late; that those Priests might as well have died then, as later. This answer is first rate stuff for poetry, but the prose fact: there was not then, nor is there living at the present day, a royal head in Europe that would not part with his crown before his life, unless honor, or the rights of others interfered. Should he make the opposite choice, I would be sorry to introduce such a stupe to any reader. These clergymen are not, and may never be, canonized; but I declare they have done the work of Saints. Those Priest-sacrifices have been undeservedly overlooked by the Catholics of America. The genius of Memphis can proudly point her finger at a congeries of martyr relics—twenty-two Priests and not less than fifty Nuns, within the precincts of her Cemetery. What other city of America, or even Europe, unless we recall the victims of the Cromwellian cruelty or the Roman persecutions, can boast of a similar repository?

It may be said the Laity of Memphis suffered as much as the Priests and Nuns. That is a false assertion. No layman or woman of Memphis was exposed as were the Priests and Sisters. With each lay individual it was only a family trouble: but the Priest had to attend to a whole parish. His mission was from house to house. When he bade farewell to one patient he had to go and close the eyes of another. This is neither poetry nor fiction.

It is a cold fact. I myself stood at the deathbedside of more than eight hundred Catholics who perished in '73. Father Aloysius, during the three plagues, must have seen more than fifteen hundred of the laity appear before God with a Yellow-Fever face. Father William Walsh, I am sure, attended as many, if not more, than myself. What laymen or women volunteered to come to Memphis during the plagues, as did the Priests who died, and the six St. Joseph nuns who left St. Louis and came to Memphis during the rage of the Fever? Point out similar laymen or women :— Doctors, Lawyers, Colonels, School teachers. One young woman of the laity, Miss Mattie Steveson, a poor but handsome girl, who left Indiana and volunteered to go to Memphis as nurse, perhaps for the sake of making an honest dollar or ten dollars a day, was immortalized—*idolized*—by the citizens of Memphis for nursing about five sick families. The citizens apportioned to her "remains" a triangular plot, over which they erected a most costly artistic monument, in Elmwood. I do not object to this. Let the people have their gods and goddesses. But neither gods nor goddesses should be overestimated. There was then many a Catholic Nun who concealed under a black veil as pretty a face as ever Miss Steveson sponged or powdered, who nursed not merely *five*, but more than *one hundred and five* families, and yet there is not as much as a cedar plank to mark her " remains."

The Sisters who had given up their mission in Memphis, but who volunteered to come from St. Louis (300 miles) to nurse the sick, received no stipulated or honorary remuneration from the citizens. Neither the Howards nor the Board of Health, nor any one of the so called Relief Committees, offered them even a vote of thanks. They had to bear their own travelling expenses to and from Memphis. But I forget. They were Religious. That abstract, *religious*, sometimes covers a multitude of the people's culpable thoughts, words and omissions.

In the high sounding style of Talmage, "The narrow-gauged course of philanthropy the Relief Committees and Howards pursued when aiding the Nuns and our Irish and Catholic people, left ample room for a double-gauged *broad* track of religious impartiality and christian charity."

To counteract the apparent rebuke which these words tend to convey, I wish to state that as Priests and Sisters are not laboring for the things of this world, they feel fully compensated by their hopes of reward hereafter, as also by the respect and loyalty of the people. If the citizens, and especially the Catholics of Memphis, should forget or ignore the sacrifice and services of the Priesthood in the darkest hour of their municipal and social existence, then I would say to them in the words of St. Chrysostom :—"*Ungrateful Christians!* is this your acknowledgment of the services the ministers of God have rendered to you? Is it not by their hands you have been regenerated in the waters of baptism? Is it not through their ministry that you received pardon for your sins? Do they not offer for you the Sacrifice which gives you the body and blood of Jesus Christ? Are they not those who instruct you, and break for your children the bread of the divine word? Who pray and open the kingdom of Heaven for you?"

Yes, Memphians, the Priests of your unfortunate city have heard the last words and messages; they have stood at the bedside and prayed and did all in their power for your loved and departed friends—in the words of the Saint, they broke for them the last bread of life, and opened the gates of Heaven for them. This is not all. They all died, or were ready and resolved to die to save the souls and relieve the bodies of your departed kindred. Other cities may fail to appreciate or admire the ordinary duties of its Priests, but let *Memphis* be silent while she venerates the memory of men who lived and died in the discharge of extraordinary duties. The graves of these departed heroes should bloom with perennial flowers. Their memories should be revered and their ashes venerated as those of veritable martyrs.

As a practical suggestion, these last remarks I consider quite unnecessary. The Catholics of Memphis have always shown the greatest respect to their clergy. In all their appeals for the erection of churches, schools and other charitable purposes, my nine years' residence in that city forces me to avow they have been most generous, and might be favorably compared with the Catholics of any other city in the United States. As long as I live, I shall never forget the noble-hearted Catholics of Memphis.

## GENERAL REMARKS.

Before concluding these "reminiscences," I trust the following general remarks will not overtask the reader's patience, in so far as they give a summary of Yellow Fever fatalities, as also a list of the important towns that contracted or escaped the contagion.

During, and long after, the epidemic, a question was mooted — Which of the two sexes, men or women, displayed the greater courage or heroism? As a direct answer might originate a domestic warfare, I feel loath to assume the responsibility of umpire in such an important question. I would much rather resume the main subject, or give a complete catalogue of all the inhabitants of each town in Tennessee, with a list of country barns, saw-mills, cotton-gins, horses, sheep, and oxen, than touch this *knotty*, or rather very *naughty* interrogatory. However, as I am now twelve hundred miles distant from the enemy's camp, I make bold to state that in regard to the attention and care of the sick, *women* displayed more courage and unwearied patience than *men*.

When the epidemic first broke out, the females, or to be more concise in my Southern courtesy, the ladies (white and colored), appeared to be the more anxious party, as they were unquestionably more tearful and clamorous. Husbands, in a few cases that I remember, either deserted their wives, or, being away, refused to visit their prostrate families. I can recollect that in two or three instances brothers left their sisters to perish, while they boarded the first train bound for the North or East. Cases where wives deserted their husbands, I failed to discover, although I am unwilling to state such desertion a moral impossibility. Indeed, there were some husbands that deserved to be forsaken, especially when during the Fever they had an opportunity of returning to a state of grace and going to heaven.

What I have said of wives, I am not prepared to affirm of unmarried ladies, dressy maidens, or female platform orators. I suppose it was their "*strength* of *mind*" that superinduced those parties to take a little "*vacation*" during the two autumns of '78 and '79. A vacation then, if not absolutely needful to recuperate lost physical energy, was most advisable, in so far as it saved the expenses of an undertaker. To this day, the undertakers view with a withering askance those fugitives that deprived them of the means Yellow Jack, by his unerring stroke, intended them to harvest. Trusting these prefatory remarks will create no ill feelings among either sex, I will now endeavor to summarize the havoc caused by the Yellow Fever during its prevalence in Memphis.

The number who died of Fever in 1873 (according to Keating's History, page 106,) was 2,000, of whom about 1,000 were Catholics. Five Priests and some twelve Nuns died this year.

In 1878, according to medical estimate, 5,150 persons died out of a population of 19,600, while 17,600 took the Fever. The mortality among the whites was 70 per cent. and among the blacks 8 per cent. Of those who died of Fever, at least 2,000 were Catholics. If we include Father Ryan, of Chattanooga, thirteen Priests and about thirty Catholic Nuns died this year.

In '79, about 800 inhabitants (of whom perhaps 400 were Catholics) died of Fever. Four Priests and some eight Nuns died this year.

During the three epidemics of '73, '78 and '79, *Memphis lost nearly 8000 of her citizens, while the Catholic population was decreased in membership about 3,400.

The office of the *Memphis Appeal* lost twenty-one members of its staff; the *Avalanche*, its editor and business manager, with fifteen of its staff; the *Evening Ledger*, although twenty-five of its members were stricken down, lost but four of its staff.

Of the Police Department, twenty-seven out of a total of forty-eight men were attacked, of whom ten died and seventeen convalesced. The dead are as follows: Captain William Homan, Sergeant James McConnell, and Patrolmen James McConnell, William Unversagt, I. J. Huber, W. H. Sweeney, M. Cannon, M. Allison, Fred. Restmeyer, and Tim. Hope.

Of the Fire Department, twenty-four men died: Capt. P. Haley, John Considine, Patrick Cronin, J. R. Luccarnia, Thomas Bren-

---

* Before the Fever of '73, the population of Memphis averaged about 55,000 and the Catholic population about 10,000.

nan, Felix Plaggio, Dennis Sullivan, Michael Fenney, Martin Carney, Michael Farrell, Tony Griffin, John Leech, Patrick Connell, R. R. Lunch, Frank Saltglamaohia, Frank Frank, John Heath, C. E. Riordan, James Hannon, Austin Beatty, Sam. Townsend, Edward Moran, Edward Lee and Thomas Heath.

Thirty-four physicians died during the epidemic of 1878: Avent, Armstrong, Beecher, Clarke, Dawson, Dickerson, Erskine, Hodges, Hopson, Bond, Bankson, Bartholomew, Burcham, Chevis, Easley, Force, Forbes, Fort, Gorrell, Harlan, Ingalls, Lowry, Otey, Rogers, Robbins, Rogers, Watson, Woodward, Hicks, Heady, Keating, Kim, McKim, McGregor.

The following table, taken from the *Memphis Appeal* of 1878, shows the progress of the disease during the climax of its prevalence:

From July 10 to Sept. 6, 1878, 958 deaths were reported.
Sept. 7...............1878, 97 " " "
Sept. 8...............1878, 99 " " "
Sept. 9...............1878, 111 " " "
Sept. 10..............1878, 99 " " "
Sept. 11..............1878, 104 " " "
Sept. 12..............1878, 98 " " "
Sept. 13..............1878, 93 " " "
Sept 14...............1878, 127 " " "
Sept. 15..............1878, 98 " " "
Sept. 16..............1878, 111 " " "
Sept. 17..............1878, 96 " " "
Sept. 18..............1878, 68 " " "

From the last date until about the 15th of October, 1878, the average death roll amounted to 50 daily.

The figures in the foregoing table by no means furnish a correct list of each day's mortality. In fact, the journal from which the figures were transcribed made this admission. When we consider that there was no special law or punishment that could be enforced during this critical time to compel undertakers to report their number of daily burials to the Board of Health, and that such an obligation, if not too onerous, was, to say the least, very annoying and unprofitable, it will be easy to comprehend how deficient the above table must be. A Memphis undertaker, after the Fever of '78, said in my presence, that he would depose on oath that on a certain day in September, '78, more than two hundred corpses were deposited in different Cemeteries. [In Keating's History it is stated that (page 147) eight thousand took the Fever in one week of September.] If we believe this statement, (assuredly no one had more actual experience,) we could almost double the figures in the tabular list. But I will not require the reader to believe the foregoing figures could be multiplied by two in order to estimate the daily mortality in Memphis; and as it would be ungenerous to misdoubt the undertaker's deposition we will simply admit the number he stated was only for one black day, to which he called special attention.

## GENERAL REMARKS. 217

In order to find out the daily number of fever-stricken patients, we will confine ourselves to the figures in the table. Let us take September 11 : one hundred and four (104) deaths were reported to the Board of Health for this day.—Sept. 14, 127 deaths—Sept. 16, 111 deaths. Omitting the first month, during which almost every one who took the Fever died, it is not unreasonable to state that during the two remaining months two out of three recovered. Assuming this hypothesis, in order to form a fair estimate of all who were attacked, we are entitled to multiply the figures of the table by three. Accordingly, for September 11, we would have 312 sick patients; for Sept. 14, 381, and for Sept. 16, 333. Now, taking into consideration the fact that the plurality of those who remained in the city were poor people, who had no means to fly from the plague and support themselves abroad for three months, and reconsidering that the greater portion of these were Catholics, who as yet form a majority of the poor white Southern inhabitants, we can form an idea of the labors of the three Priests who had to attend to almost all the sick calls of the city and two Camps. I say *almost all*, for the reason that the Priests who fell took the disease after the first, second or third exposure. On Sept. 14, there must have been at least 300 sick calls, thus affording 100 calls for each Priest.

After this very judicious division of day and night work, I think New-England clergymen need not complain of being overburdened with sick "calls."

Hearing a young Priest of this locality ask me with animation to guess how many sick persons he attended one day last Summer, I could scarcely conceal a smile when he averred that he attended *nine sick calls!*

I trust the reader will not consider it a vain boast when I state that in October of '73, I visited one hundred sick persons in one day. This would be quite impossible were I obliged to go to separate houses. In a boarding-house, corner of Front and Market streets, facing the river, I anointed by *one repetition* of the ritual "form," ten persons in the same room. I feel convinced that the Priests who attended the fever-stricken in Memphis in '78, (Fathers Kelly, Aloysius and Walsh,) could enumerate a larger record. It was out of the question for a Priest to think of returning home to take meals during the crisis of the scourge. A morsel, placed before him by friends on his way, was all he could expect. Although the parishioners were very reasonable regarding night "calls," still, sudden, if not injudicious or intemperate "calls," obliged the Memphis Priest to keep his eyes wide awake.

Having reluctantly made use of the pronoun I, in the preceding examples, I would plead immunity from egotism or vanity, when I declare I have had no other motive save that of recording the unvarnished truth. As I have never held pretensions to extraordinary zeal in the exercise of my "calling," I simply state that I only did my duty for the time, and that were any other Priest of the diocese in my place, he would have done as well—perhaps a great deal better.

As I have insinuated, the facts I relate are known to at least fifteen thousand people in Memphis and throughout the State of Tennessee ; I now beg to state that rather than maliciously indite misstatements regarding persons or events, I would unhesitatingly burn this manuscript. I do not say this book contains all indubitable facts. "*Humanum est errare.*" I would simply state that while inditing the work, I really meant to record the truth and nothing but the truth.

Begging the reader's pardon for this diversion, I will now resume the rest of the subject as promised in the "General Remarks."

The following are the principal cities, towns and villages, besides Memphis, where Yellow Fever appeared in '78 :—Chattanooga, [300].

The figures in brackets show the distance from Memphis. Father P. Ryan, who died of Fever in '78, was resident pastor of this city. Present population, 12,892. Brownsville, [57], attended by Father P. O'Brien, present pastor of Lake View, Chicago; present population, 2,475. Humboldt, [87], attended by Father O'Brien, had a few cases (isolated) of Fever; population 1,636. Milan, [93], attended by Father O'Brien, had also a few isolated fever cases; population, 1,693. McEwen City, [175] attended by Rev. John Fahey; population 300. Grand Junction, [52], attended by Rev. P. O'Brien; population 450. Paris, [131], population 1,800, had several cases of Fever; attended by Rev. D. A. Quinn. Covington, [37], population 100; attended by Rev. D. A. Quinn. Several smaller towns—Shelby, [19], Mason, [36], Stanton, [44], Kerrville, [20], Germantown, [15], Moscow, [31], suffered from the Fever of '78. In the State of Arkansas, opposite Memphis, Hopefield, [2], and Mound City, [5], attended by Father William Walsh, were decimated by the Fever.

CITIES AND TOWNS THAT ESCAPED THE FEVER.

NASHVILLE.—The largest city of Tennessee that escaped the Fever, is the capital of the State, Nashville, having a population of more than fifty thousand. It appeared miraculous that this city should escape, being in the centre of the State and surrounded on all sides by towns ravaged by the Plague. Although Nashville had heretofore been the rival of Memphis in wealth and population, she generously received all Memphis refugees and harbored the orphans sent from the latter town, many of whom had the Fever. This beautiful little city is indeed entitled to the gratitude of Memphians for the philanthropy and christian charity she extended during the darkest days of their municipal existence. At present there are four catholic churches within the city limits: the Cathedral, Assumption Church (German), St. Joseph's, West Nashville, and St. Columba's, East Nashville. The Catholic population of the city may be estimated at ten thousand. For Catholic schools and educational institutions, Nashville is not only a model for southern, but for many larger northern cities of greater pretensions. Besides four parish schools and a college for boys, there are two select female Academies. St. Bernard's, under the direction of the Sisters of Mercy, stands within a few hundred yards of the Cathedral, and under the shadow of the State Capitol—the latter said to be the third finest State structure in America. The parish school, also conducted by the Sisters of Mercy, is situated opposite the Capitol and within a few hundred feet of the Academy. This church property is of enormous value, being in the heart of the city and surrounded by marble mansions valued by thousands of dollars a foot. About six hundred children attend the Cathedral parish school.

St. Cecilia's Academy, or in conformity to more æsthetic parlance, St. Cecilia's Young Ladies' *Seminary*, under the conduct of the Sisters of St. Dominic, has been for the past twenty years the favorite "Alma Mater" of many of the prominent ladies of different creeds and nationalities, hailing from Tennessee, Kentucky, Alabama, the two Carolinas, and Georgia. The horse-cars accommodate passengers almost as far as the Seminary, which is itself a magnificent building, enclosing an area of some ten acres. Would that the inmates of Vassar had the bright laughing faces of the young ladies of this institution.

In Nashville there is also a most commodious orphan asylum under the management of the Dominican Sisters, who, besides boarding and clothing, give a salutary education to some four hundred waifs.

It is a noteworthy fact that the Catholics of Nashville, without resorting to fairs, picnics, bazaars, or other obsolete church money-making devices, voluntarily contribute four thousand dollars annually for the support of their orphans. Waiving further reference to the charities and church progress of Nashville, I will endeavor to give the reader a cursory view of its physical aspect.

The Post Office, on Broad street, composed of white Tennessee marble, if we except the Capitol, is the finest public building in the State. All the chief streets and thoroughfares, at night, are illuminated by electric lamps swung from circular arches. A costly suspension bridge spans the Cumberland river, that divides East Nashville from the city. The Vanderbilt and Fisk Universities, whose erection cost millions of dollars, adorn the suburbs of West Nashville. That which this thriving city wants most—its greatest, its almost intellectual want—is a city park. It is strange that such a wealthy and refined people should overlook such an addition to their many other civic advantages, while they are content to gaze upon the murky walls of the "Old Market House," which, it seems, is the only obstacle to such an enterprise.

The city of Nashville is built upon, and surrounded by, rocky hills. Almost in the heart of the city there is a beautiful sulphur spring, whose curative properties have been approved by some of its best physicians. The

Cumberland, although itself a commodious and pretty stream, occasionally causes great damage to houses and lumber located near its banks. In 1882, when the river had risen to its highest water-mark, I remember attending a sick merchant named Doherty, residing in College, a central, and one of the finest streets of the city. To reach his house, I and the physician had to take a skiff, in order to enter the second story window of his residence, which was submerged in twelve feet of water. The gentleman is still living, and remembers with pleasure this eventful episode. Notwithstanding this little queen city gets a casual surf-bath, this fact does not dampen the ardor of the citizens, who claim for Nashville the sobriquet of "*Rose*" or "*Rock*" city. Indeed, every one who visits Nashville is bound to favor her pretensions to cleanliness and beauty. On the pinnacle of her capitol, Nashville could plant a flag emblazoned with the words: "No Yellow Fever spore can enter this Burgh." On the flag-staff, however, it would not be out of place to pencil: "Rock citizens! Beware of Cholera!"

KNOXVILLE [450].—Population, 15,000; Pastor in '78, as also at present, Rev. Francis Marron.

CLARKSVILLE [199].—This little town, having a population of 6,000, displayed much philanthropy during the Fever panics. Several refugees from Memphis, one of whom had a genuine case of Yellow Fever, were allowed to enter. The citizens displayed far more courage and liberality than could be seen elsewhere throughout the State. Rev. P. J. Gleason was Pastor here during the epidemics. Rev. A. Vaghi is at present Pastor. Although the Catholics in this little town do not outnumber one hundred families, they can boast having one of the finest Catholic churches in the State, besides a parish school and select academy, in charge of the Sisters of Charity, being a branch of the house of Nazareth, Ky. All modern improvements— water-works, street railroads, and gas-works— accommodate the citizens. Messrs. S. and M. Sullivan, Parlin, Abbott, Boylan, Nolan and Dennehy are true Catholics in every sense.

JACKSON [100].—The inhabitants of Jackson, numbering about 6,000, pretend their city, as second-class, is far superior to Clarksville in wealth, population, and municipal prestige. For tourists and strangers, the best policy is to let the Jacksonites enjoy their civic vanity, for it must be remembered they are the people who inaugurated the shot-gun reign during the Fevers of '78 and '79; who broke a parlor stove, fearing it contained a spore of small-pox; and who, if a bird or four-footed brute came from Memphis during fever-quarantine, would either shoot or have it disinfected three miles outside the city limits. There is a Catholic church in Jackson, erected by the late Rev. E. Doyle, who died in '79. It also has a select academy and parish school. The present Pastor is a Rev. Timothy Abbott. Should Yellow Fever ever invade Jackson, and this clergyman pass unscathed its quarantine regulations and by-laws, he ought to be promoted a *mitred Abbot.* I trust it will not incite the spirit of envy, when I mention among the exceptionally good Catholics of Jackson, Judge Freeman (a convert) and his excellent lady: Messrs. McMullen, Carr and Cunningham.

All the Priests who attended the Fever-stricken, during the Memphis epidemics, have either died or left the diocese, except Rev. William Walsh, Pastor St. Bridget's church; Rev. A. Luiselli, Pastor St. Joseph's church; and Rev. John Veale, Pastor St. Patrick's, who attended some Fever cases in '73.

In addition to the irreparable shock which cholera and Yellow Fever epidemics imparted to the physical and financial prosperity of the city, the progress of Catholicity, after the panic had subsided, was destined to receive another crushing stroke. I refer to the order from Rome enjoining Right Rev. P. A. Feehan to resign his charge in Nashville, and assume the more exalted dignity, the Archiepiscopate of Chicago. If this promotion (which his talents, prudence and zeal justly merited) contributed to the prestige of Chicago, the consequent orbitude of the diocese of Nashville was equivalently depressing.

From the 10th of September, 1880, until the 24th of June, 1883, (almost three years) the diocese of Nashville was left without a Bishop. It is true an Administrator was appointed to govern during the interval, but this Reverend old gentleman found the task of healing the wounds of an impecunious and afflicted diocese impracticable. It required a man of *unquestionable ability* to resume the crozier which the late Bishop had laid aside. At length, after long and anxious suspense, it pleased the authorities in Rome to appoint a successor to Bishop Feehan. Although it may appear audacious of me to give an opinion as to the relative merits of men in every sense my superiors, yet as the subject requires some reference, I do not hesitate to state that the promotion to the See of Nashville of Right Rev. Joseph Rademacher was most eligible and opportune. Having been called from his large and wealthy pastorate in Lafayette, Indiana, he has been deservedly credited with more than ordinary prudence, religious zeal and financial ability.

This young Bishop was born in Clinton Co., Mich., December 3, 1840. He made his classical, philosophical and theological studies at St. Vincent's College, Westmoreland Co., and at St. Michael's Seminary, near Pittsburg, Pa. He was ordained in the Cathedral of Fort Wayne, Ind., August 2, 1863. During eight years he was Pastor of St. Mary's chapel, Fort Wayne, and for three years Pastor of St. Mary's, Lafayette, Ind., when he was consecrated Bishop of Nashville, 24th June, 1883. Although he appears younger than most of the Priests of his diocese, he possesses the experience and executive ability of older heads in the Episcopacy. Though his surname, (Rademacher, wheelwright), may do violence to the DENTAL *defects* of some of our old Irish people, his pleasing face and affable manners will win their hearts. Since his advent to the State, the Catholics of Tennessee appear to be gaining courage and forgetting their past misfortunes. His demeanor towards Priests and people is admitted to be highly satisfactory, while his every-day increasing popularity threatens to outrival the fame of his illustrious predecessor. May no clouds of early sorrow blanch his saintly countenance; may he never have cause to regret his mission among the clergy and Catholic laity of the diocese.

In conclusion, I would implore the God of Mercies to accept the innocent blood of the martyr Priests and People, as a propitiatory sacrifice; to withhold the scourge of his wrath and spare poor Memphis from a repetition of her past disasters. Amen.

# YELLOW FEVER.

The Yellow Fever, or as Dowell prefers to term it, *febris typhus icterodes*, or *febris cum nigro vomito*, or *fievere jaune*, of the French, and *nigro vomito* from the Spanish, was known to the Caribs, according to Breton, who wrote in 1655, by the French "*coup de barre*," expressive of the muscular pains of the Fever, as if produced by blows from a stick.

The visitations of Yellow Fever to this and other countries, whether epidemic or not, so far as any record of them has been preserved, follow in regular sequence, its origin, causes, methods and means of propagation, and of transmission, diagnosis, and cure. It has never made its appearance in Asia nor in Australia, nor in any of the islands of the Pacific Ocean; and it has only been felt sporadically on the Pacific coast of North and South America. In Europe, it has invaded Spain, Portugal, Italy, France and England. In South America, it has prevailed in British Guiana, Columbia, Peru, Bolivia, Buenos Ayres, and the Brazils. In North America, it has invaded Honduras, Mexico, all the West India Islands, Canada, and the following States of the Union: Maine, Vermont, Massachusetts, Rhode Island, New Hampshire, Connecticut, New Jersey, Pennsylvania, New York, Delaware, Maryland, Illinois, Indiana, Missouri, Ohio, Kentucky, West Virginia, Virginia, North Carolina, South Carolina, Georgia, Alabama, Tennessee, Mississippi, Arkansas, Louisiana, Florida, Texas; also the Indian Territory. It is said to have originated in Africa, but of this we know nothing. The following treatise on Yellow Fever, taken from Neil and Smith's Analytical Compendium of Medicine, is a reliable thesis :

## YELLOW FEVER.

Syn.—Typhus Icterodes.—Bulam Fever.—Vomito negro.—Vomito Prieto.

This is a disease of warm climates, depending upon a special cause, occurring mostly during the summer months and ceasing on the appearance of frost. It is met with chiefly in towns upon the seaboard, or upon streams emptying into the ocean.

*Symptoms.*—The attack may or may not be preceded by prodromic symptoms, very often coming on without any warning, and occurring in the midst of ordinary health. It is generally ushered in with a chill and severe pain in the back and limbs. After febrile reaction has been established, the skin is hot and dry, the respiration hurried, the face flushed, the eyes red and watery, and the conjunctiva much injected. There is a sense of uneasiness, sometimes tenderness, at the epigastrium, accompanied by nausea and vomiting. The tongue is at first moist, and covered with a yellowish-white fur; there is also extreme thirst. The pulse ranges from the natural standard to 120° or even 140°. Sometimes it is unnaturally slow; either extreme is significant of great danger. Sometimes there are delirium and prostration; at others, the mind is clear, and the muscular strength unimpaired. The bowels are ordinarily costive, and when the discharges are obtained, they are commonly unhealthy in character. As the disease advances the pain in the limbs becomes more intense, especially in the lower extremities, the calves and front of the legs. This stage is called by some authors *the stage of invasion*, and lasts from a few hours to three days; the shorter the duration, the more violent, generally, is the disease.

After this comes the stage of remission, or, as it is sometimes called, *stage without fever*. All the symptoms abate, and the patient seems to be convalescent; there are symptoms present, however, by which the experienced are warned of the continuance of the disease. It is not the same as the remission of bilious fever, but is produced by the exhaustion of the powers of the system. The epigastrium is even more tender upon pressure, the skin becomes yellow or orange color, the urine assumes a yellow tinge, and the pulse sometimes sinks as low as forty in the minute. After a short calm the stomach assumes its former irritability, and the peculiar substance called *black vomit* is ejected. The tongue is dry, brown, and chapped. The patient becomes more and more prostrated; there are, at times, passive hemorrhages, at others, suppression of urine, or retention. The pulse becomes more and more feeble, the respiration sighing, the matter ejected from the stomach is brought up without effort, and discharges of the same matter take place from the bowels. This stage is sometimes called *the stage of collapse*. Sometimes, instead of collapse, symptoms of reaction set in, which are always to be regarded as a salutary effort of nature, sometimes terminating in health, sometimes, however, running on to extreme exhaustion, or assuming a typhoid form.

*Anatomical characters.*—The membranes of the brain are often found injected, and serum effused into the ventricles. The stomach usually presents traces of inflammation, having its mucous coat either reddened, thickened, softened, or eroded. The peculiar matter called black vomit, is now generally believed to be blood altered by admixture with the acid secretion of the stomach. The liver is altered in color and consistence. According to Dr. J. Hastings, late of the U. S. N., it resembles old boxwood in color, and is much harder than natural. Sometimes it is dry and anæmic, though rarely inflamed. It varies in color from a lemon-yellow to a straw color, and in consistence, from being soft and friable to positive induration. It often presents evidence of fatty degeneration.

*Cause.*—Speculation is rife as to the cause of this disease. There is no doubt that it is as specific as that of small pox, though of its precise nature nothing definite is known. Heat and filth, alone, are not able to produce it; neither are marsh miasmata, independently of other causes. The idea that it is owing to the same cause as that which produces remittent fever, is erroneous; for in many parts of the world where the latter disease is constantly occurring, yellow fever has never been known; again; yellow fever especially prevails in large towns; this is not the case with remittent fever. Acclimated persons are very seldom attacked with yellow fever, while it is well known that one attack of bilious fever secures no exemption from another. Nor are the symptoms of the two diseases alike: the first stage of yellow fever is continuous for one, two, or three days, while bilious fever remits from the first. As regards its contagiousness the weight of evidence and authority is divided. Dixon believes it to be contagious and portable. Others deny it altogether. Strangers are more liable to it than long residents, and whites more than negroes. Among the predisposing causes are exposure, intemperance, fear, and sudden changes of the weather.

*Diagnosis.*—At first it is not easy. As the disease advances, however, the severe pains in the back and lower extremities, the peculiar injection of the conjunctiva, the excessive irritability of the stomach, the yellowness of the skin, and finally black vomit, are enough to diagnosticate the disease.

*Prognosis.*—Generally regarded as unfavorable, though much depends upon the person attacked, the character of the epidemic, and the severity of the symptoms. Symptoms of great prostration are very unfavorable, and a total suppression of urine is certainly a fatal sign. Stranguary, however, is regarded as a favorable sign.

*Treatment.*—Early in the disease, before there is much

irritability of stomach, an emetic is of great service, particularly if the stomach be loaded; it should only be used, however, under these circumstances. Bloodletting, to be of service, should be employed early, and even then not unless called for by the violence of the symptoms and state of the pulse. Cold affusion is highly recommended. Mercurials are, on all sides, declared to be of great service in this disease. They should be administered, first, with a view to their cathartic action, and then to their specific influence, as rapidly as possible. Febrifuge medicines are also called for; of these, perhaps none is so good as ice given internally, together with cool sponging externally—the latter with caution. Ice often allays the irritability of the stomach. To the same end, the effervescing draught may be employed, and sinapsisms or leeches externally. If the pain in the head is very great, cups or leeches may be employed, together with cold applications to the part. In the second stage, the febrifuge and depleting remedies should be suspended, except the mercurials, to which may be added the acetate of lead, with a view of diminishing the inflammation of the stomach, and also for its astringent properties. Blisters may also be applied to the epigastrium and the raw surface sprinkled with acetate of morphia. The muriated tincture of iron is highly recommended, in doses from 20 to 60 drops every two hours. Its administration should be commenced before the black vomit appears. Acetate of lead has also been found useful given early. In the third stage, cordials and stimulants are demanded. Sulphate of quinia, infusions of bark, or serpentaria, carb. of ammonia, capsicum, turpentine, wine whey, or brandy and water, may be administered. External stimulants, such as frictions, sinapisms, hot baths, etc., may also be found beneficial. The apartment should be kept well ventilated, and all excrementitious matters removed.

# A SYNOPSIS

OF

# Missionary Life in Eastern Arkansas.

From 1874 to 1878, while I chose Memphis my place of residence, I had charge of Missions located in four States, embracing a territory subdivided into twenty-three counties—a district unquestionably larger than all Ireland.

The following counties in Tennessee: Fayette, Hardeman, Tipton, Lauderdale, Crockett, Dyer, Gibson, Obion, Lake, and a part of Shelby. [10.]

In Arkansas: Crittendon, Crosse, St. Francis, Mississippi, Craighead, Poinsett, Prairie and Woodruff. [8.]

In Mississippi: De Soto, and a part of Tunica and Marshall counties. [3.]

In southern Missouri: Pemiscott and Dunklin counties. [2.]

As the country missions in Tennessee, Mississippi and southern Missouri are not very unlike those in northern or western States, I shall not detain the reader by any detailed account of their hardships or facilities. My object in referring to them at all is simply to show the scarcity of Priests and the paucity of Catholics throughout these regions. Lest I should incur the taunt of egotism, I beg the reader to excuse, in the subsequent narrative, the frequent repetition of the pronoun I, which cannot be eschewed without seriously detracting from the import of what I write.

The following are the towns and villages of eastern Arkansas I had to attend for four years: Hopefield [2]. The figures in brackets denote in miles the distance from Memphis. Mound City [5], Marion [14], Edmonson [17], Madison [41], Forest City [45], Palestine [52], Brinkley [70], De Vall's Bluff [87], Carlisle [103], Osceola [90], Gayosa [100], Kennet [110], Wittsburg [60].

As a medical doctor cannot ply his craft without the needful instruments, drugs, and vulnerary appliances, for graver reasons the spiritual physician must bring with him everything necessary for the decent administration of the Sacraments and the cure of souls. I shall preface my synopsis with a list of a missionary's complete outfit.

A PRIEST'S MISSIONARY VALISE.

A valise available for the country missions should be of bivalve formation : one section reserved for ecclesiastical, and the other for secular appurtenances. The ecclesiastical bi-partition should contain: an altar-stone, chalice, paten, crucifix, missal and stand, (vestments, one color for all occasions), chasuble, maniple, stole, cincture, alb, amice, cassock, burse, with three purificators, corporal and pall, chalice-covering, three altar-linens, finger-towel, three altar-cards, one papal prayer, altar wine, altar breads (large and small), a pair of army candlesticks with two candles, ritual, purple stole, breviary, book of epistles and gospels, a little bell, three sermons, (lectures if possible). (The Bishop of Tennessee required a stole and surplice for the administration of the last Sacraments.) With the above, should also be carefully packed a number of rosary-beads, scapulars, agnus Deis, and lace pictures; near which should be orderly shelved, a baptismal registry, a number of catechisms, polemic tracts, and a sufficient number of controversial works, such as the Faith of our Fathers, Catholic Belief, Why am I a Catholic, etc., etc. The Missionary should never forget to bring, about his person, a pix and replenished oil stocks, and a small vial of baptismal water.

The secular division of the valise should contain three or four days' supply of Graham crackers, a patent alcohol stove, with supply, small tea or coffee pot, a can of beef, a fan to ward off the mosquitoes, and a bottle of pennyroyal to banish midnight vampires. After all these things are systematically adjusted, there will be plenty of room for a moderate variety of under-clothing, hose, handkerchiefs, towels, gents' toilet and dressing case, collars, cuffs, matches, stationery, etc. Itinerant Preachers generally provide themselves with a revolver or shot gun, to guard against wild animals or robbers; but as a Priest would become irregular were he to shed human blood, he is not expected to carry firearms, either in his pocket or valise. If the missionary should have piscatorial propensities, he should fasten to the outer straps of his valise a patent fishing-rod, with a capacious umbrella, impervious to rain or sunshine. Charged with this portmanteau, the young missionary might go forth to combat the *Powers* of *Darkness*, and evangelize the benighted natives scattered through the prairies, forests and swamps of Arkansas.

It may be urged that some of the abovementioned articles might be dispensed with.

I grant that in missions where vestments, chalice, etc., are preserved in the church, and where catholic families afford accommodation for the Priest, several of the above-mentioned articles might be left out; but while attending the missions of eastern Arkansas, the

Priest could not overlook any of the above-mentioned details. Is there anything in the ecclesiastical portion a Priest could conscientiously omit? It may be said that rosary beads, scapulars and pictures might be excluded. I can assure the reader these things are anxiously besought by the country folk, and contribute to preserve the faith in those who might otherwise become lukewarm or apostate. Referring to the secular division of the valise I beg to state, that it is not for the sake of enlarging the list that I have mentioned so many articles apparently supernumerary. I can aver I seldom or never failed to bring with me on the missions a valise containing all of the above-mentioned appurtenances, and being in delicate health, I had also to provide myself with medicines and other necessary restoratives. I assure the reader that should a Priest fail to bring those missionary adjuncts, besides having his night or day's rest disturbed, he would invariably find his stomach as well as his purse, very slender, before he returned to his central habitation. Besides being guided by memory, his judgment should suggest to have the altar-stone and luggage as light as possible, in order to facilitate their carriage from and to the depot or steamboat landing. It sometimes happened that an Irishman at hand would proffer to bring the Priest's valise; occasionally he would be invited to take breakfast or dinner with some catholic family; but as these were mostly all poor through the missions of Arkansas, such chances were rather exceptional. I remember once, while crossing the Devall's Bluff Prairie, the villainous horse which I rode gave a sudden plunge and upset me and the valise I held on his back. As the brute scampered away, seemingly delighted at being relieved of his burden, I had to shoulder my baggage in the midst of a scorching summer's day, as far as the neighboring woods, a distance of four miles. I then learned how much more expedite it was to have transferred to saddlebags the contents of my valise, while attending missions on horseback. Unless an annual "free pass" were given, a Priest could not, without being financially destitute, attend any of the missions in eastern Arkansas.

### HOPEFIELD, MARION AND MOUND CITY.

The town of Hopefield, in the County of Crittendon, and State of Arkansas, is situated opposite Memphis. It is quite unnecessary for tourists or landlopers to know its latitude and longitude; this information is indispensable only to steamboat captains and rivermen, who during a part of the spring and fall have to rely on the compass and sun in order to find out its position in the map of the world. Hopefield is not the chief city, for in size and population it is second to Marion, the Capital of Crittendon county. Mound City ranks next to Hopefield in commercial importance, as also in its similar advantage, being built on the river. Within the city limits, covering an area of one square mile, (in 1878) there were eleven houses, three of which were lager-beer saloons, and all the rest boarding-houses, except one, which appropriated the title:—"Hopefield Tavern." [Several railroad men boarded here.]

In the early part of '78, one Stephen McNeil, an Irish resident of Little Rock, donated me a portion of the suburbs of Hopefield for the purpose of erecting a church thereon. As the Catholics of this town had always been very liberal, their offerings enabled me to build a church thirty feet long, sixteen feet wide and twelve feet high. This church, to which I shall again make reference, was dedicated with due solemnity by the Bishop of Little Rock, a few weeks before the Yellow Fever appeared in Memphis, in 1878.

Although the Mississippi separates the two cities, Memphis conveyed a case of Fever to Hopefield that was unmistakeably genuine, and which the poor "Democrats" working on the railroad declared was the only *genuine* "article" Memphis ever shipped to Hopefield. The little town was more than decimated. Jerry Stack and wife, Mike Guttery and wife, a Mrs. O'Keeffe, and several others (R. I. P.) the Yellow Fever caused to cross a deeper and wider River than the Mississippi. Only one Catholic family survived the epidemic. This sad fact induced me to write to the Bishop for permission to sell the church. He consented. Although the building had cost five hundred, it was sold for one hundred dollars to a Mr. John Leonard, who afterwards sold it to negroes, who now hold their midnight orgies in it.

The reader may be surprised that suburban property so near the thriving city of Memphis should be sold for such a small amount. This surprise will vanish when I state that, unless to some enterprising restaurateur who might make great profit by the sale of mud-turtles, eels, and bullfrogs, no one else would give five hundred dollars for the whole county of Crittendon. I would be sorry, and would positively refuse to act, should some deceased relative appoint me sole executor of Hopefield, Mound City, or Marion, the Capital of the county.

Some one may ask—Have I anything good

to say of Hopefield? Yes! the few Catholics that lived and died there shall ever have a "remembrance" in my humble prayers. In justice to the town itself, I am willing to admit that not even Paris, London or New York reveals the creative bounties of Providence more vividly than Hopefield, Mound City or Marion, seen through a mosquito-canopy or a microscope. The Memphis & Little Rock and Memphis & Kansas railroads have their termini in Hopefield, from which the trains are conveyed to and from Memphis on ferryboats. The inhabitants entertain the notion that at some future day a great iron bridge will span the river, and thus make Hopefield another East St. Louis. My suspicions are quite contrary. Should the Mississippi be bridged over at Memphis during the present century, I have no doubt Hopefield would be entirely ignored. Before Hopefield can expect to compete with East St. Louis or Brooklyn, the entire county of Crittendon should be lifted at least twenty feet above its present barometrical elevation.*

Meanwhile, let our best wishes favor the ecclesiastical, political and commercial prosperity of Hopefield, Marion and Mound City.

*In 1811, an earthquake lowered the region of country about New Madrid (bordering on Crittendon county) ten feet below its previous level. The depression was so great that the rivers flowing into the Mississippi turned back against their source.—*Scribner's Magazine for March, 1887.*

## FOREST CITY, BRINKLEY, OSCEOLA AND OTHER MISSIONS.

Fearing that a detailed description of the other towns located on the missionary district apportioned to me, may prove uninteresting, if not tedious to the reader, I shall simply refer to them in a general way. The Missions in Tennessee and Kentucky assume an attitude of civil enterprise nearly equal if not similar to that of Northern States. The Missions in Arkansas are primitive, and hitherto I have not seen any description that has done justice to their originality. The inhabitants, Catholic and Protestant, the churches, the towns, the railroads, and the very *waters* themselves, all appear to be different from what you would expect to find elsewhere. On the walls of some of the country churches you read in large Roman letters: "Please avoid talking and spitting;" "No lady or gentleman will spit on the floor," &c. The bayous and sluices, instead of flowing towards the river, as even the course of nature would seem to facilitate, in Arkansas run directly from the river, (see "Mississippi" in Appleton's Encyclopedia.)

The first time I celebrated Mass in Arkansas, I felt I was dealing with a very singular part of the globe. Hence, while narrating some ludicrous things, I fear I have to assume a tone of hilarity rather unbeseeming a man of my years, yet, were I to overlook them, I could not verify my promise to furnish a "graphic" account of the Missions.

Referring to my first Mass in Arkansas, during the service, or manner of serving, (which of course I could not change,) an improvised choir, accompanied by an old piano, violin and flute, shouted glory to the church triumphant in Heaven, while they seemed to have no regard for the church "tortured" on earth. On the occasion of a church benefit to procure an Altar, I was amazed to find that a hurdy-gurdy and a hand-organ formed the only "musicale" that delighted the audience. The hand-organ repertory was exhausted only when it squealed out "The wind that shook the barley."

In the church of Forest City, a lady who generally had her protestant husband accompany her, seldom suffered the Priest to finish his discourse until she had interrupted him two or three times. In the midst of his sermon he often had to explain to this good lady what the church meant by indulgences, the use of images, the veneration of the Blessed Virgin, and the Infallibility (not Impeccability) of the Pope.

When entering a country boarding house

in Arkansas, the first thing a Priest should do is to take off his hat. This simple act of politeness, while highly gratifying to the Catholics, affords a pleasing surprise to the unbelieving country "folk," who heretofore imagined every Priest had two horns on his forehead. Indeed, a tumor on the temple of a certain Bishop has excited a good deal of suspicion in this regard. This prejudice would appear inexplicable if we did not consider the confused notion which those benighted people have on the occasion of the installation of a Bishop, who must receive "the Bulls" before he can be ratified a Roman emissary. Such notions are gradually becoming obsolete, but there is no doubting the fact of their having been entertained, and even to the present day suspected by a certain low class of natives. The many unfounded prejudices that the people have been taught to believe regarding the Pope and Priests, the Confessional, and other doctrines of the church, seriously mar the progress of Catholicity in these regions. During the several years of my missionary life in Arkansas, I must say I never met a Protestant who had correct notions of the Catholic church. On the contrary, they often harbored opinions that are monstrous, if not blasphemous.

Besides the church of Osceola, on the Mississippi, I had to attend to three churches which I erected on the Little Rock R. R. at Hopefield, Forest City and Brinkley, besides all the interjacent little villages between Memphis and Carlisle. The Missions on this Railroad were most arduous and destructive to health. (I feel convinced that they materially contributed to ruin my constitution and superinduce the two paralytic "shocks" which have left me almost an invalid for life.)

As there were often more than a thousand men employed on the railroad, (invariably all Catholics), the Priest was expected to say Mass at least every two months in each section house along the line. I had to hear the men's confessions generally on Saturday evenings, when they had quited work, and give them Holy Communion the following morning. In winter, as I awoke in the morning, I often found my bed and bedding entirely covered with snow. The huts wherein the men slept, being built of rough logs, were not impervious to rain or snow. Mr. Martin Kelly, a prominent railroad contractor, still living in Memphis, remembers when he frequently endeavored to stuff the chinks of our little log cabin on the six mile trestle.

In winter, the huts occupied by the section men were insufficiently heated. Having frequently remained over night in these cabins,

I found it necessary to wear my overcoat and keep pacing the floor of my sleeping compartment until morning. Even when the sun had arisen, I often felt so cold that in order to keep my blood in circulation, I used to walk from Edmonson to the twenty-three mile bayou and return, a distance of twelve miles. During the worst days of winter, it was no uncommon sight to find railroad men almost to their knees in puddle, while in summer the drinking water was so distasteful and stagnant that it had to be saturated with lime or rice.

The trains of the Little Rock railroad, as I shall show later on, seldom during those years ('74–'78) observed schedule time. In truth, a weather-bulletin was more reliable than a train moving East or West on this road. I often had to remain eight, and sometimes twelve hours of nights stretched on the cold floor of a wretched depot-room, and very often adjacent to *colored*, and those still more unsavory expectorant country "folk," awaiting a due train.

In addition to cold, the cravings of an empty stomach often tested human endurance. I remember spending a certain Christmas day at Brinkley, Ark. I was obliged to hear several confessions, say three Masses and preach. My Christmas collection amounted to forty cents. Breakfast at half-past one, P. M., consisted of a cup of coffee without sugar or milk, which I cooked myself, and a loaf of dry bread, which a little girl (named Mollie Dorsey) left for me in the Sacristy. Some one will ask, why did not the Catholics invite me? I repeated the same question to myself. Although there were three or four catholic families living near the church, it appeared nobody's business; besides, a Priest in the possession of a forty-cent collection could afford to go to a hotel.

As I have no desire to cast obloquy on the Catholics of this town, I simply state, by way of exoneration, that, as there was a very rich Catholic in the town, all the others imagined I was invited to his house. Between them all, Santa Claus gave me a very bare branch of the Christmas tree that morning.

In each of the three churches I erected, I took care that a portion of the building was partitioned into a little room, wherein were placed a bed and stove. The Priest, when tired, could come here and lie down without disturbing or being disturbed by domestic inmates. In saying *being disturbed*, I do not mean so much the screaming of implacable babes, or the noise in the barn or kitchen, as the more intimate and itching disturbance beneath the bed covering. I will refer to this as soon as I devote a few lines to the native Arkansas mosquito. Perhaps, of all the living things around, he is the most attentive to business. Once inside the canopy (or mosquito-bar, as it is called in the South,) there is but one infallible way of putting an end to his venomous piping—simply to set a match to the mosquito-bar. Any other device will only infuriate the little creature, that is sure to draw some of your best blood before morning. St. Paul gives a sad recital of his "persecutions," "shipwrecks," and wonderful "escapes," but, except the flaggellations alone, I would venture to undergo all the others rather than remain one night a helpless victim to a swarm of Arkansas mosquitoes. Even cows, sheep, and horses do not escape their venomous rapacity. You might almost see them coming into life, as they cover the stagnant waters of the swamps for a distance of sixty miles.

Although the mosquito tantalizes during the long sleepless nights, still the unseen enemy of man's nightly repose—the bug—is yet more tormenting. Besides, as their presence, unlike mosquitoes, bespeaks a want of vigilant housewifery, a gentleman—especially a clergyman—cannot complain of those nasty vampires. Although I have no desire to dilate on this unseemly subject, still, I must say that during the years I attended the Missions on the swamps of Arkansas, all my other privations and sufferings did not equal the tortures those vile creatures caused me. As the rats and mice which I often had to encounter at night never caused me personal injury, I became accustomed to their squealings and nocturnal rompings. I would rather be surrounded by an army of those untamed rodents than remain passive to the odor and blood-sucking rapacity of one bug. Rather than sleep in beds I knew infested with them, I often remained in the train all night, and came back on its return trip the next morning.

I mention these trials, not for the sake of arrogating self-credit therefrom, but with the view of inducing young Bishops having charge of missionary dioceses to be slow in mapping out a rural district, whose regular attendance calls for superhuman hardships, and often ruins the health of the visiting clergyman. I know many learned and zealous Priests who, for seven, and even ten years, have been attending most arduous Missions throughout Kentucky, Mississippi and other southern States, while others, having college titles prefixed or affixed to their names, escape all undesirable exposure, as they nestle around the Cathedral or some large city church. Although I have the greatest respect for such dignitaries, still I think it would not soil their repute to labor a little while in the thorny portion of the Lord's vineyard. As the swarthy husbandman should not always be denied the flowers and fruit he cultivates, so the poor missionary should be relieved from his arduous labors before he is disabled by age or infirmity.

Although it may appear audacious, I honestly believe no Priest should be suffered to remain more than four years on any isolated mission as long as there is another who has not been on the missions, residing in the diocese. It may be urged that some Priests are naturally and intellectually more suitable for the city than the country missions. I grant the drift of popular surmise favors this hypothesis. However, as all catholic clergymen must complete a regular college course before ordination, I consider this *natural* or *intellectual* aptitude an artificial subterfuge rather than a passable argument. Many think that, while a man of ordinary parts would suit the country, a polished and gifted one should be retained in the city. Experience proves the contrary. The city Priest seldom or never meets any one that will dispute his doctrine, calling, or revenue. His person and his words are considered sacred. The country missionary has everywhere to defend his church and doctrine. Unlike his city brother, who will receive his pew-rents and church-dues with obsequious courtesy and without preaching, or after any Mass, high or low, the missionary must preach a good sermon if he would have a pleased audience and a good collection. If the people give what they very often gave me, a very poor collection for my very poor services, the Priest must either do better the next time or starve, or else give up the missions. Of course, a Priest has motives higher than this groveling pursuit, but, after all, the most elevated dignitary, besides being decently clothed, must eat and sleep—functions which require a moderate expenditure of the poor missionary's coppers. The city Priest's bed and board are generally prepared at his own direction; the country missionary has no right to order anything special for his meals (being supposed to have a patent stomach), while he is expected to express much thanks for the room and couch that are assigned to him. A talented and highly accomplished young clergyman, when he leaves college, should not be suffered to have the repository of those gifts tainted by the murky atmosphere of a large city. The fresh air of the country, for at least three years, is just the stimulative for him.

Again, there is another difficulty with the missions. In many rural districts or small towns, prominent members of society who have a greater readiness to wield the pen than open the purse, frequently address to the Bishop of the diocese glowing letters full of promises which the Priest to his cost finds they never fulfil. Apprised of this fact, (I have been informed) that Most. Rev. Archbishop Elder, while Bishop of Natchez, as also Bishop Fitzgerald, of Little Rock, when making their annual tours through their dioceses, used to tell the country people they should not apply for the regular attendance of a Priest unless they contributed ten dollars at his every visit. This was but just and reasonable, in view of the fact that Priests are frequently called sixty, and sometimes one hundred miles from home, either to attend the sick, marry or baptize, after which, sometimes, their fares are not offered to them.

In the few remaining pages, I will endeavor to delineate some of the features of the topography of that portion of Arkansas that lies between Memphis and Little Rock, with a brief reference to its inhabitants and railroad enterprise, which I trust will not be uninteresting to New Englanders and the people of other States.

## AN ARKANSAS QUAGMIRE.

It must be remembered that when the Mississippi overflows its banks, or rather natural bed, (as to sodden banks, they do not exist, except in the brains of White-House candidates) animals of the forest—such as bears, wolves, panthers, deer, coons and possums, of all which a variety roam through the surrounding woods—must betake themselves to the interior as the waters advance. In their daily and nightly migrations, several are drowned, or perish with hunger or fatigue. Then, the fishes that leave the river-bed proceed miles into the country. When the waters subside, the carcasses of millions of these creatures may be seen decaying during the summer and autumn months. If you add to this debris, decayed leaves, plants, and vegetables, you will have a superficial picture of an Arkansas swamp. As the country is mostly virgin forest, the sun cannot reach a tenth part of all this decomposed matter. It is a peculiarity of the Mississippi to be continually swallowing up the land that encroaches on its waters. Trees, forests, and sometimes entire villages, are submerged in this manner. It is curious, and almost painful, to see the entire sinewy roots of huge trees exposed to view, and waiting for their doom. In some localities, where the river has risen high, the steamboats, which a few weeks before landed a half a mile away, come right up to the farm houses. I have known families who had to remain several weeks in the second story of their dwellings, waiting for the waters to subside.

I recollect staying over night in a little town in the northern portion of the State, bordering on the Mississippi river. Having slept at a friend's house, I saw, as I awoke in the morning, a great steamboat coming right towards the house. I considered it prudent, not only to expedite, but to postpone all toilet service not absolutely necessary. Before I had time to go down stairs, the steamboat had already jammed against the house. The shock was soon over; but the gentle little jostle the house received was a potent "reminder" that, if that domicile did not look out or leave the steamboat's way, her bowsprit next time might split it asunder. Ropes and telegraph wires fastened to the ground secure many a dwelling house between New Madrid and Vicksburg. In fact, there is record of a whole village which has entirely disappeared from the banks of the river. I remember when the steamboat wharf at Napoleon (1867) was a mile from the Catholic church. [This church, by the way, was ransacked by the Yankees, the natives say. The bell was dragged down from the steeple. I saw myself on the broken plaster where a soldier fired his gun at the crucifix over the altar. An Irish soldier killed the miscreant on the spot.] This church, the court-house— the entire village, are now buried in the river.

### THE LITTLE ROCK RAILROAD, AS IT APPEARED FROM 1869 TO 1878.

A glance over a map of the United States will show that Little Rock is almost directly due west of Memphis (133 miles). The Little Rock Railroad connects the two cities. This road had been for more than twenty years in process of erection. I mention its process of erection, because the only thing to be done, and which seemed never could be done, was to keep the road-bed above the surrounding dump or mud. Forty-one miles of this road, from Memphis to Madison, were, and still are, in the midst of a virescent swamp. It took the train three and sometimes four hours to crawl over these forty-one miles. The train that left Memphis at half-past three P. M. was supposed to have made good schedule time when it reached Little Rock at half-past twelve next morning. If it had not to pass over two prairies, where it sped at the rate of forty miles an hour, it could not possibly reach Little Rock in less than twenty hours. Stepping off the cars, and looking at the road-bed, it appeared thus:

if, in addition to the linear, you also include concave and convex, zigzag, tortuous twistings of the rails. As the road had never been approved, passengers had to take their own risks. It being the only direct road to Texas and the West, the trains were always crowded, notwithstanding the delay that might be expected. If a solid bottom could have been reached, a double track would be a paying investment. But this seemed impossible, when we consider that, for the previous twenty years, a thousand men, more or less, had been engaged repairing it, without any visible signs of progress.

In one part of the road, there were six miles of continuous trestle. When a train fell through, as it frequently did, it was amusing to hear the wits and wags quizzing and gibing the Company and Officers of the road. Actors and preachers having special appointments were remarkably eloquent in their denunciations. One cold winter's night, there was a "smash-up" in the woods near Black-Fish station. It took fifteen hours to repair the road. The passengers had to go into the forest. For fires, they piled railroad ties and great decaying logs that lay scattered around. As there was no inhabited house nearer than six or eight miles, wild hogs, coons and possums were roasted in the turf and soon devoured. The ladies, who at first were ashamed to admit they were hungry, might be seen gradually becoming more familiar. Before the train was ready to move, they were very glad to eat or drink anything that was offered to them. I saw several parties eating raw cabbage; and the worst of it, the brakeman fought till he was overpowered to prevent even this. Although I will not vouch its accuracy, a conductor told me that on several occasions passengers would go into the woods, shoot down a wild turkey or a coon, and then leisurely overtake the train. While the locomotive was puffing with all its might, I often got off myself, walked several hundred yards and afterwards found no difficulty in stepping on the platform of the hindmost passenger coach. On another occasion, I was in the rear caboose, when twenty-two freight cars were dashed into the woods, although the train was not going faster than eight miles an hour. Cows, horses, and a car-load of hunting dogs afforded a strange sight. The plaintive howling of the imprisoned and wounded dogs was an evident sign they did not appreciate, or at least anticipate the capabilities of the Little Rock railroad.

I recall another event which, although bordering on the miraculous, was very amusing. Some twenty-five miles from Memphis, a train loaded with cattle and emigrants (both were often conveyed on the same train) was nearing a trestle-bridge some twenty feet high, when all of a sudden a mule got on the track. The engineer immediately whistled down brakes, for next to a "wild engine," a mule to an average railroad man is the greatest terror. Before the train could stop, the engine struck the mule, and immediately jumped the track, about fifty yards from the trestle-bridge. By what appeared a miraculous intervention of Providence, the flange of the driving-wheel bumped over the cross-ties a distance of two hundred feet, and within one inch of the extreme edge of the trestle. Had the engine fallen over this frightful chasm, besides the engineer and fireman being scalded alive, it is almost certain that half the people on the train would be mangled to pieces. I noticed hardened old travellers turn pale as they reviewed the long line of deep indentures made by the driving-wheel. Having just crossed the bridge, the locomotive, eight or ten box-cars, and three passenger coaches toppled over. On the cow-catcher, a tramp was stealing a ride. He was literally buried in the mud. It took some ten section men over an hour to dig him out. The poor fellow was not even hurt. When good humor was restored, all the passengers crowded around the tramp. One passenger (a Jew) told the tramp to sue the company; another dryly remarked he had better first seek a soap factory and hose. At all events, the poor fellow was glad to have escaped with his life. As for the poor mule, his blood and bones were promiscuously scattered for several hundred yards on either side of the track. If, in the slang of Josh Billings, he intended to "demolish" the train, the train "demolished" him badly. But the surprise of this narrative is not yet ended. A stranger would imagine it should take a week to get this engine and those cars on the track again. You will scarcely believe—the train and section men had the locomotive and coaches replaced on the main track in less than five hours. A small side-track was improvised. By means of hydraulic jacks and other implements (which were always carried for such contingencies), and a wrecking engine, the locomotive and cars were lifted out of the puddle and replaced on the track. From the nonchalance of the conductor, I presumed he scarcely considered it necessary to report to the company such a *trifling* accident. On either side of the railroad, between Hopefield and Argenta, might be seen the rust-eaten ruins of locomotives and the rotting debris of demolished cars,—each of which told the story of a ludicrous accident or an awful catastrophe.

It was no unusual occurrence on this railroad for several years, that passengers should have to await a due train three, five, and sometimes fifteen hours. Even then, the passengers had no scheduled guarantee or seasonable hope that might allay their anxiety. If the trucks did not bump the traveller off his seat, they would assuredly keep him constantly agitated. In this respect, a New York Broadway buss was a half a century ahead of a passenger coach on the Little Rock railroad. If there were not thousands of persons living who have witnessed many of the facts I relate, it would appear incredible that a train passing over this short distance would get off the track once, twice, and frequently four times during a single trip.

Lest the preceding remarks should tend to discourage traffic over this very popular railroad, I would recall to the reader the heading of this article, which simply proposed to give a description of the road as it appeared from the year 1869 to '78. Even when the road was in its worst condition, human life was seldom jeopardized, owing to the fact that the rate of speed over the swamps did not exceed eight, and frequently not more than four miles an hour. The railroad company and not the public suffered most from daily mishaps.

During these years ('69 to '78) a passenger might see an approaching train which he wanted to "board" a thousand yards distant, but neither engineer, conductor, nor telegraph agent could afford him the least assurance as to what was going to happen before he would have occasion to produce his ticket. The train might pass over the thousand yards of swamp safely; it might jump the track; or a pair of trucks might break over the tortuous rails; or it might (what was often as annoying) switch* for an approching train, or "wood up,"—a task which generally required half an hour. Indeed, I often heard a conductor abruptly answer a "green" traveller's inquiry, "that nobody in that place politely called 'Gehenna' in the 'revised' edition, could tell when the train would get to Memphis."

I have no doubt but this road at present is complete, in which event it will be, for its length, the most popular railroad in the Southern States.

---

*It frequently happened that a passenger or freight train would *side* track for a due train two and sometimes five hours.

## INHABITANTS OF THE SWAMPS.

On both sides of the railroad you see through the open car windows snakes of every size and variety, basking in the sunshine, or coiled up on decayed logs or the stumps of old trees, while countless numbers might be seen slouching in the mire, or wiggling in the water, with now and then a "copper," or "black-head," protruding. Some gentlemen-travellers take great delight in firing off their revolvers through the windows at these defiant uplifted heads. I do not remember to have ever seen one killed by the most steady marksman. The water moccasin and "copper-head" are said to be the most poisonous. A passenger, one day as the train stopped to take in wood, attacked a huge rattlesnake as he lay stretched between the rails. He aimed a blow with a long stick, which broke, as he failed to hit the snake. All of an instant the snake coiled himself into a round, ball and erected his tremulous head and forked fangs. His little eyes were sparkling with fire. As the gentleman flung at him the remaining portion of the stick, with an elastic bound the creature flung himself towards his assailant, and had he not quickly ran back might have cause to rue his temerity. As the train whistled to move we could hear the viper rattling defiance. Besides snakes, might also be seen mud turtles, (some as long and wide as an ordinary door) toads, eels and catfish, wallowing in the mire. Catholics from the East, travelling through those regions on Friday, often sigh for the fish-pots of Cape Cod and Provincetown, while they feast an empty stomach with the recollected flavor of scallops, oyster stew, and clambakes.

While furnishing the reader with a detailed account of venomous flies and crawling vampires, I would be doing great injustice to the fecundity of the Arkansas swamps were I to overlook the superabundance of another species of reptiles. Stepping off the cars at any railroad station on the Little Rock Railroad, above the howling of wolves, the barking of prairie-dogs and the hissing of snakes, you will hear, if not very euphonious, at least very distinct noise. The creatures that cause this, though once of *classic* fame, at present do not rank very high among the upper "ten" of high toned vocalists. Like many of our modern church choristers, if their voices are not appreciated they take good care and precaution they shall be heard. I would be loath to mention their names in this category, were I not convinced these creatures' phonetic capabilities have been undeservedly underrated. I trust I will not overtask the reader's patience while I direct his attention to the myriads of toads and bull-frogs that make the air resound with their discordant croakings. Passing by the toads, the Arkansas bull-frog deserves especial notice. This creature's body, though not very graceful, is assuredly well developed. There is no laconic stretch of imagination in saying that the roar of a lion or a veritable bull would not resound so far as the deep groaning of this amphibious little prodigy. When I first heard the sonorous basso of the creature, I asked a woodman what wild animal made that terrible noise. When he informed me, I really thought he was bantering: I did not believe him then, and would not afterwards had not several other foresters repeated the same assurance.

IRISH IMMIGRANTS IN EASTERN ARKANSAS.

There is many a poor Irish Catholic family living in these benighted regions. In the wildest woods and prairies of Arkansas, Mississippi and Missouri, our people are scattered. In twenty counties of Arkansas, where I travelled, I always found an Irishman or an Irish family. Eight, ten, and fifty miles from Priest or church, still the faith was living and strong. Nine miles from De Vall's Bluff, on the prairie, bordering an immense forest, lived a poor Irishman by name Boland. His wife was a graduate of the Convent of Dubuque, and her father there is a wealthy farmer. His son-in-law having saved a couple thousand dollars (being an excellent carpenter as well as farmer), took a notion to emigrate to Arkansas. He bought a thousand acres, at fifty cents an acre, of this half prairie, half woodland. He, like many others, thought he would, in a short time, make a great fortune. To the eye, this prairie land seems to be as rich and fertile as the prairies of Illinois or Iowa. But after a year or two, the poor farmer sees he was wofully mistaken. For corn and wheat, those prairies are a decided failure. Boland worked like a giant for two years. He wrote to Bishop Fitzgerald, begging him to send a priest to baptize his two infants. The latter requested me to visit him. I ventured to find, or rather to hunt him up. Getting off the train at De Vall's Bluff, I hired a horse to carry me to the place where it was supposed this Boland lived. As I rode along, I passed many a herd of deer and several wolves or prairie dogs. At last, having reached the edge of the forest, I came to an impassable creek. I had to swim the horse over it —a resort new, and very disagreeable to me at the time. Driving along a foot-path, or as woodsmen say, a "trail," for about a quarter of a mile, I heard a noise or echo, as though some one was felling a tree. I rode in the direction. At last I came to an open plot, which revealed that portion of Boland's farm he had cleared and reclaimed. Sure enough—there was Boland himself, stripped to the waist, with well poised axe, making the air resound with his hardy blows. Seeing me at a distance, he ran, seized my hands and kissed them; then leading my horse, conducted me to his house.

It was a wretched log cabin, entirely erected by himself and wife. We entered the house. There was the wife, with a babe in her arms. She began to weep when she saw me; they were tears of joy. Kneeling on the floor, she raised her eyes to heaven, and thanked the good God for having sent a Priest at last. The babe looked up, too, but perhaps it was only to its mother. She asked me for God's sake to remain a week, as she had not seen a Priest since she left home, and had not seen a white man for several weeks. I did not, for his wife's sake, wish to alarm poor Boland; otherwise, I would have asked, why, in God's name, did he bring this delicate woman, with her babes, to this, if not God-forsaken, at least man-forgotten, wilderness? Next morning, I said Mass in their cabin. It would move the most hardened person to see this poor fellow kneeling, his big, brawny and bleeding hands being clasped in fervent prayer. Beside him knelt his wife, clutching her two babes, while she occasionally raised her tear-fraught eyes to heaven. The children, in their mute behavior, looked as though they were little angels. Having no carpet, the poor woman insisted I should stand on her shawl whilst saying Mass. I felt as though the first Mass said in that virgin ,forest was the grandest sacrifice of my life. For dinner, we had prairie chicken and wild deer, which Boland had killed the day before. The *saddest feature,*—the poor man was enthused with chimeras of the future paradise he was determined to create. Ah! he little dreamt, as I then surmised, that sickness and poverty would soon drive him penniless from that wretched wilderness.

I remained with Boland two days. I can never forget my departure. The wife and children and poor Boland himself were audibly weeping—fearing, perhaps, they would never live to see a Priest again. I have lost trace of this man for the past five years. I trust he is now living with his respected father-in-law in Dubuque, Iowa.

Another respectable family by the name of Noon, attracted by railroad pamphlets and land agents' advertisements, moved to this part of the country. Mr. Noon purchased 150 acres of reclaimed land four miles north the little town of Carlisle, Arkansas. Although no Catholic church or school is within thirty miles of the place, he settled here with his family. After testing all the resources of manual labor and industry, he saw that his little store of reserved funds was growing less and less. At length he became discouraged, sold his farm and returned to his former home in Bristol, R. I. After preaching a sermon in the Catholic church of Bristol, last December, (1886) I was more than surprised when an elderly lady called to see me at the parsonage, and asked me if I were the Father Quinn that celebrated Mass at her house in Carlisle, Ark. I could hardly believe any Irish family from New England would have courage enough to settle in that dreary wilderness. The good lady, however, soon convinced me that she and her family emigrated to, lived in, and all but one returned safely from, the forests of Arkansas. The solitary exception was her young and beautiful daughter Maggie, (14 years old) whom, as she expressed it, a "*Hoosier* made away with."

Another immigrant, from Illinois, a Mr. Manning, purchased several hundred acres in another part of Arkansas, known as the Goodwin Prairie. He, too, came with a firm belief that the prairie lands of Arkansas were as productive as those of his native State. Like most immigrants, he selected for his future homestead a place where prairie and woodland adjoin, with the view of having fencing and building materials, more accessible. In one respect, Manning was more fortunate than Boland. He had seven stalwart sons. Brinkley, where the nearest Catholic church stood, was eight miles distant. During a considerable part of the year the road was impassable; still, he was seldom absent, notwithstanding he had often to wade his way through snow and slush. When I last heard from him, five years ago, he and his brave boys were still fighting the forest, or rather wasting their young lives in this unprofitable and assuredly most unhealthy soil. Such isolated Irish families as the above are scattered almost throughout every county of Arkansas. Their condition is especially deplorable, not generally because they have to fight and fail in the wilderness, but because they are beyond the reach of church, school, or common civilization.

### THE "HOOSIER" OR COUNTRY NATIVE ARKANSIAN.

There are a few, and only a *few* eligible cities in Arkansas. Little Rock, the capital, with some 16,000 inhabitants, is a beautiful city. Hot Springs and Fort Smith come next. After these, Pine Bluff, to Arkansians, is, or will soon be, an empire city. But to outsiders, Pine Bluff, like Jackson, Tennessee, is nestled in the midst of a loathsome swamp. All the other towns and villages of Arkansas, put together, would not congregate as many people as the city of Louisville, Ky.; while in appearance this hypothetical city would not look as well as Louisville sunk four stories into the earth. In Little Rock, Hot Springs, Helena, Fort Smith, and Pine Bluff, there are some very intelligent people. In fact, most of the villages of the State having a population more than a thousand are like other cities, having an average mixture of citizens—good and bad, wise and foolish, virtuous and disreputable. But take the country native;—for a low type of Caucasian humanity, I might challenge the world, not for his equal—for he has no incarnate stereotype—but for a specimen several grades above this anomalism. Although the people of the State of Indiana have a prior claim to the sobriquet of "Hoosiers," still, the country Arkansian, when designated from his city brother, is always called "the *Hoosier.*"

When I first saw a group of those creatures (I do not refer to Indians), I began to speculate which of the twelve tribes of Israel emigrated to Arkansas. It is true this native has a soul, and the Catholic church has an anxious eye after it. But while speaking of his soul with the greatest respect, I beg to state the Arkansian Hoosier's body is a pitiful wreck of humanity. It is the color of the clay on which he stands. I have seen them *dipping* snuff and eating *clay.* Some allow the latter is used as a substitute for gum, but I was assured there is a certain quality of clay which they actually swallow.

I was once in the caboose of a freight train where there were some five or six of those country "folk." As the train passed Forest City, they ran to the side door to see what they never had seen before—a *brick house.* I had occasion to remember this event, for one of them stood on my foot, in his anxiety to see the modern marvel. Seeing me wince at the pain, he apologized, saying: "Boss, skuse me; but that there house takes me all hollow." As they had occasion to cross the Mississippi in the transfer-boat, which took the train over to Memphis, a boy about nineteen years old poked his head through the window as a steamboat was passing. While a big navy revolver protruded through his hip pocket, he cried out: "O, *ma,* see how she *puffs!*"

From personal acquaintance, I must say these natives are innocent and honest. Their notions of the Catholic church, in some cases, are very ludicrous. The Bishop of Little Rock dedicated a church in Forest City some seven years ago. During the week, I met one of those country Hoosiers.—tall, lank, and lazy-looking. "Parson," said he, "I understand the Pope is coming to Forest City next week." I told him the Pope could hardly reach Forest City by Sunday, but that the Bishop would surely be there. "Who is that?" he asked. Accommodating myself to his crude notions, I told him the Bishop was the "Boss" of all the Priests and Catholics of the State. "Well," continued he, "I don't know as I'll come to see the Bishop. I'd like to see the Pope; I hard a good deal of that old gentleman." A section foreman afterwards told me this old fellow was present at the dedication. He was so "skeered" that he would only enter as far as the church door. With distended eyes, he watched the Bishop, robed in full pontificals. On the occasion of the mitre being placed on the Bishop's head, he nudged his comrade, saying, "O, Lord! Jake, what a hat!"

This might appear to some a story made up for effect, but Priests who attend missions in the South have often experienced more outlandish things.

A Mr. Dowling, an Irishman who operated

a flour mill in Friendship, is still living to testify the fact that once, while I was putting on the several vestments used at Mass, an old lady started for the door. On the assurance of Dowling that I had no more garments to put on, she was persuaded to remain. This old lady's fear, like many others, was founded on the prejudice that a Priest was a kind of necromancer, who, by dexterous manœuvres and change of vesture, could cast a spell on those around him. You hear of Irish and English who, to their sorrow, and sometimes shame, can neither read nor write, but the average American backwoodsman does not know that the three R's are civil accomplishments.

I remember once being announced to *lecture* (preaching was beneath the standard) in a little country town near the boundary limits of Missouri. As the place was about eight miles distant from the hotel wherein I boarded the previous night, I hired a horse, and was kindly accompanied by a medical doctor, who was the bearer of the invitation. Long before we reached the town, my name was heralded for miles around. Even the little village paper issued an *extra* on the occasion.

As we drew near the town, we could see several young and old, male and female heads protruding through the windows and broken panes of the distant houses,—I suppose for the purpose of seeing what they had never seen before, a Catholic Priest. It was in the middle of summer. In the evening, the bell of the Baptist church rang out for more than an hour, the warning for the "lecture." When all had assembled, the little church was so crowded that I had difficulty in forcing an entrance. As the window sashes were all taken out, I could see a far larger multitude peering through the windows than the congregation that sat before me.

Making use of the pulpit and Bible provided for the occasion, and having announced the text, I had just begun to get into a vein of pertinent thoughts, when, to my disgust, my ancient church enemy—a sickly or froward babe—began to scream. Seeing the infant had monopolized the attention of the audience, and fearing that during the course of the lecture I was likely to have a very persistent rival, I quietly requested the mother to take the little one to the door, or into the open air, until it would become quiet. She paid no attention to my appeal. I proceeded, but soon felt that the baby was several notes higher than I could reach. I again requested the mother to leave the church. [She sat on a front bench.] This time she did not pretend to notice me. After another effort, I suddenly ceased to speak, and gazed at the congregation.

Being aware that there were not more than three Catholics among the audience, I considered a reserved course the more prudent. In most unassuming words, I appealed to the congregation, requesting to know their preference of orators, myself or the baby. From suppressed whispers in several quarters I could judge that they preferred to hear me for the time. The lady in question seemed to acknowledge this, also, for she, with her three sisters who sat near, immediately stood up, and with angry faces left the church for their homes. I then resumed my lecture, and although introducing the blessed Virgin, the Pope, and the Confessional, I received marked attention. In fact, a committee of some twenty gentlemen called to see me before I left the church, and requested me to remain with them a week, assuring me I would have more than one convert amongst them. As I had made other engagements, I could not accede to their wishes. The next day I was invited by the Doctor who accompanied me to dine at the house of a respectable resident of the place. I cheerfully promised to do so; but just as I had finished grace and sat down to table, to my amazement, whom did I recognize opposite me but the three sisters and the mother whom I had ordered out of church. To make my predicament more embarrassing, I was informed she was my hostess. I apologized with all the jarring phrases a guilty man generally makes use of. The lady told me not to be in the least disturbed. "Although I was a bit angry with you at first," she said, "myself and the girls got sorry and went back again." On our way home, the Doctor who accompanied me called at a drug store on the roadside, some two miles from the village we had just left. As soon as he entered, I noticed the proprietor walked from behind the counter and went out the rear door. During his absence, I could hear the Doctor rummaging among bottles under the counter. On our way home, as we quietly jogged along, I asked the Doctor why the proprietor left the counter as soon as he entered. With a cunning wink he informed me that as both were members of the "Temperance Brotherhood" their constitution obliged them to report a defaulting member; so the other gentleman left in order that he might have no cause of complaint. In the course of our journey homeward the Doctor recognized an old country farmer whom we met on the way. After shaking hands and exchanging several rustic pleasantries, the Doctor asked the farmer for a "chew." The old farmer appeared to be perfectly scandalized. "Why, Dr. H——!" he exclaimed, "I thought you belonged to the *church.*" The Doctor hung down his head, completely non-plussed. Casting a look of sympathy at myself, the farmer said: "Parson, I fear you have a very profane companion." Hitherto, although I was aware that writing, fishing, or playing the piano on the *Sabbath*, had been regarded an unpardonable sacrilege by the country "folk"; this was the first time I was made to understand chewing was considered a *licentious desecration.*

When we had arrived in the little town of C—— the Doctor insisted on my staying over night with himself. I consented. As I entered his house, or rather his wretched log cabin, he introduced me with the most obsequious formality to his three sons and daughter. The oldest son first came forward; "Reverend Father," said he, "this is my son, Horace—Horace, this is the Reverend Father Q——." He then afforded me the pleasure of shaking his hand. Milton, with hair combed back, and adorned with a profusion of pomade and curls, came next. "Reverend Father, this is my son Milton—Milton, this is the Catholic Priest." This gentleman also graciously gave me his hand. The next was introduced in like manner. Last of all, came the father's pet, Rosetta. Before all men, even ministers, every specimen of the fair sex hold a prior place in Southern non-Catholic society; hence the form of introduction was inverted in favor of Rosetta. "My daughter Rosetta, this is the Priest." She simply made a profound courtesy and assumed all the dignity of a virgin queen as she sat on an adjacent stool. The room in which this lavish display of etiquette took place consisted of four wooden chairs, a table, a stove, three beds, and a shot gun. The Doctor left, apologising that he had some patients to see before night. In his absence, the oldest son told me to make myself perfectly *at home.* He then asked me if I needed any refreshment. I cordially agreed to accept all that he could furnish. With all the inherited dignity of his father, he went out into the yard, and approaching an old oaken bucket, he returned with a gourd filled with fresh water. Being very thirsty, I was pleased to accept the proffered refreshment.

In an opposite garden, enclosed by a very high latticed fence, I noticed a countless number of poultry:—geese, turkeys, ducks and chickens. I asked Horace why they kept so much fowl. Standing up, with a genteel courtesy he said: "Reverend Father, the people around here are very poor; there is no money amongst them, so Pa has to exchange his practice for poultry." He then resumed his seat, while Rosetta's cheeks revealed a modest blush. At night, when the Doctor returned, he and I occupied the same room. As he was called up about three o'clock to visit a patient, he assured me I would not be disturbed till morning. This pleased me very much, as I was very tired and anxious to sleep. As I awoke about eight o'clock, I was keenly mortified to notice the door and four windows of my room quite open, without any screen or curtain. The people on the sidewalks, and even in the adjacent houses could, (and no doubt did see me for several hours) lying in bed. Even as I resumed my clothes and cassock, I discovered two little urchins peeping through the chinks, in their curiosity to see a Priest.

The reader may think it ungenerous, if not ungrateful, to expose to ridicule the domestic habits of those who, in their limited way befriended me. In the first place, I would state in reply, that I have said nothing untrue or damaging to the parties; secondly, I have industriously substituted fictitious names, while the locality where this scene took place is as difficult to be explored as would be the task of discovering a family simply addressed "Massachusetts," or "Connecticut." If I did not introduce a few such examples, I could not keep my promise to the reader to furnish a "graphic account of Arkansas missionary life."

On the following Monday morning I left the Doctor's house to celebrate Mass in the Masonic hall, which was kindly tendered to me. The building was crowded with Catholics and Protestants. I dispensed holy communion to twenty-five persons. It was really edifying to see young and old, men and women, with their beads and prayer-books which some had not used in church during ten previous years, kneeling with profound reverence, and audibly worshipping God. Some fifteen of those who had received the sacraments had ridden on horseback over ten miles, through swamps and thorny brushwood, fasting. Amongst the latter was an enfeebled mother, sheltering her six months old babe. Their religious zeal and love of God might appropriately stand a rebuke to those lukewarm Catholics whom a little rain or cold will prevent going to Mass, even while living almost under the shadow of the church. As our Lord said of the centurion, I could truthfully say of those good people: "Such great *faith* I never witnessed during my missionary experience."

Not only Priests, but even Bishops, in the South, have often encountered such ludicrous adventures as those I have narrated. The present Archbishop of Chicago, when Bishop of Nashville, (I trust his Grace will not feel wounded by my reference to his name) had often to experience very embarrassing difficulties while making his Episcopal visits through the country. I remember on the occasion of his administering Confirmation in middle Tennessee, where he had to sleep in a room not larger than eight feet square. He being of a gigantic stature could almost touch the ceiling with his head. The room was so hot (in the midst of summer) that he could scarcely retain his ecclesiastical garments.

I was once heartily amused, especially when I saw no possibility of averting the annoyance (the mother being present), when little unkempt country boys and girls jumped on his knees, toyed with his hat and watch-chain, searched his pockets, and abruptly asked him for a nickel.

As I have already insinuated, a Catholic Bishop or Priest, before a real Southern non-Catholic lady, has no social or civil rights, except through her expressed permission. It would be considered very rude to lower or lift a window, to sit down to table or leave it, or to wear the hat on, without the lady's consent. If a young lady, besides a rug and shawl, had a score of parcels, the *gentleman*, even though he were far advanced in consumption, must carry them all. [Of course an *old woman* would be *permitted* to carry those things herself; whilst a blind or decrepit person is generally left in charge of the brakeman.]

I remember once seeing a clergyman (I do not smoke myself) light a cigar at the rear end of a L. & N. passenger coach, which was entirely empty, with the exception of a puny little specimen of the sex at the further end. He had scarcely drawn two whiffs when the little lady screamed out "*Conductor!*" The conductor hurriedly responded. She said in some sort of a key outside the natural scale that "some *gentleman* was smoking in the car!" The conductor came up and ordered him to cease smoking in the *ladies'* car. Had I not known this clergyman dearly loved his mother, his chagrin was so bitter I could imgine he wished that old "Adam" was never burdened with the presence of a "lady."

A patron of Delmonico's would appear an uncouth monster were he to sit down to table and nonchalantly call for his bill of fare before he had previously washed his face and hands and adjusted his hair and whiskers. To act otherwise would be an unpardonable breach of Arkansian etiquette, although in many instances there would be more sediment in the water than in the complexion.

Domestic osculation is another feature of Arkansas country life. If there were thirteen little boys and girls going to school, or to the cotton fields, each one is obliged to kiss *father* and *mother* before leaving and after returning. Even old, gray-bearded *Pa* (pronounced paw) has to give *Ma* her morning and evening salute, though the latter may sometimes be in an *oscitant* rather than an osculant disposition.

### THE HOG THAT ATTEMPTED TO UPSET THE CHURCH OF BRINKLEY.

Although the two following anecdotes may appear to be rather puerile, still, as they are founded on fact, and furnish an occasion to give a scathing rebuke to a certain class of church members, I trust the reader will not be distressed at my recital.

In the new little church of Brinkley (chiefly erected through the munificence of Messrs. Gunn and Black) there was a room 8x6 feet, set apart for the Priest's sleeping apartment. Right opposite was a Sacristy of similar dimensions. The Sanctuary divided the two rooms. Very early one fine Sunday morning, as I lay on the little pallet, which was prepared (or rather which I prepared myself), I was startled out of a pleasant nap by a violent upheaval of the floor and bed on which I lay. The presence of an earthquake at once occurred to me. I made the sign of the cross and repeated an act of perfect contrition. The vibration soon after ceased, and I consoled myself with the hope that it might be a *century* before anything similar would again occur. My *centenary* calculation, however, was soon falsified. Just as I began to nap again, my little bed began to describe an acute angle, and soon after a semi-circle; and as far as physical elevation counted, I was lifted higher in the church than ever I had been before in my life. Considering this promotion too sudden to last long, I immediately jumped out of bed, and went directly out before the little altar, where I knelt and extemporized the best prayers of my life, for then I was preparing for what I considered inevitable death. I owed a few little *bills*, and wished from my soul I had paid them before I crossed the river Styx. I awaited the dread yawn of nature to engulf me. But, thank God! I was mistaken in my fears. Nature and the little church remained very quiet, until I returned to my pallet again. This time I was not kept long in suspense, and was thoroughly undeceived. A gentle snort from an imprisoned huge "Porcus" beneath the floor allayed all my forebodings.

Two years after, when I was given charge of St. Patrick's parish in Memphis, finding among my good people some very meddlesome parishioners, I bethought myself of the hog that endeavored to upset the church of Brinkley.

> "Give me the avowed, the erect, the manly foe;
> Bold I can meet—perhaps may turn his blow;
> But of all plagues, good Heaven, thy wrath can send,
> Save, save, Oh! save me from thy candid friend."
> —*Canning.*

### THE WOODPECKER.

One fine Easter Sunday morning as I lay on the afore-mentioned pallet in Brinkley, after the manner of my favorite author, Edgar A. Poe, I heard a "rapping" and a gentle "tapping" at the opposite sacristy door. Thinking it was caused by some poor country "folk," or laborers on the railroad who wanted to go to confession, in order that they might fulfil the Easter obligations by receiving holy communion that morning, I called out to the parties to "wait a moment." I got up, hastily put on my cassock and crossed over the Sanctuary to the Sacristy. As I unlocked the door I expected to see the parties who rapped. To my surprise, I failed to see any one although it was a bright moonlight morning. I called out, but got no answer. Although I did not experience the mental agony caused by the imaginary earthquake, I began to think of ghosts and midnight robbers. I went back to my room, looked at my watch, and was surprised to find it was but half past two, A. M. As I was very tired, having been seven hours on the train the evening before, I returned to my couch and was enjoying a good nap, when all of a sudden the "*rapping*" and "*tapping*" began again. As the building was a new frame structure, the noise seemed to shake the whole church. Requesting the parties to "wait a moment," I jumped up and immediately ran to open the door. Again I was nonplussed. Not a soul or body could I see.

"Deep into the darkness peering, long I stood there, wondering, fearing,
But the silence was unbroken, and the stillness gave no token."

Being piqued at such disappointment, I resolved to see what it was—*man* or *demon*. Holding the knob, I gently closed the door to await the next rap. I did not have to wait long. On hearing the first tap, I immediately flung the door wide open, when to my surprise and disgust a villainous woodpecker, with a scream, flew away and perched on a neighboring tree. Remembering that I should say Mass in a few hours after, I abstained from wishing my intruder more inconvenience than he caused me. Years after, when I was located in Memphis, and was called to see ladies and others whose presence was announced by the violent ringing of the door-bell of the parsonage, and finding they had little or no business, I could never refrain from thinking of the little *woodpecker* that caused me so much annoyance, although I had never wronged him or any of his family in my life.

During my sojournings amongst the rural inhabitants of Arkansas, I often had to yield to the strange and ludicrous feeling of hearing myself addressed in all manner of titles, ecclesiastical, professional, military and civic. Almost every new acquaintance had another title for me. Judge, professor, squire, although familiarly used, were not as frequently prefixed to my name as colonel or captain; while parson, brother, or priest Quinn, was the usual form of address by those who believed in the "Church." In rustic Arkansian vocabulary, to "believe in the Church," simply meant any form of belief in God. I never found a native Arkansian (unbelievers, of course) that seemed reconciled to the Catholic custom of addressing a Priest, "Father." In some cases it did noticeable violence to their outward respect for a friendly young Priest when some senile member of either sex accosted him in a "Fatherly" capacity. The spiritual sense in which it is used by Catholics appeared to be something which they could not, or at least did not wish to comprehend.

Although I consider my personal remarks sufficiently intelligible, yet, before concluding these reminiscences, I would preclude the possibility of misconception in my reference to the native inhabitants of Arkansas.

I have stated that in large towns and cities the people's manners, customs and morals were not very different from, if not equal to, those of northern or eastern cities. In candor, I must acknowledge I have found native American Arkansians (with whom I have had a long and thorough acquaintance) some of the choice specimens of man and womanhood. They have proven themselves intelligent, religious, and strictly honest and honorable. My uncomplimentary remarks must be taken as referring only to those benighted natives that are born and bred in the wild prairies, forests or swamps of Arkansas, far away from the influence of church, school, or civic intercourse. These poor people have had no opportunity to ameliorate their physical or social condition; and, unless I would speak falsely, I must give them credit for having kept within the narrow limits of their social privations. The few preachers, or so-called *ministers* of the *Gospel*, that go amongst them only serve to confuse or confirm them in their ancient prejudices.

During their autumn revivals and camp-meetings I have known hundreds whom I saw go into the waters and embrace the baptist faith, at the next conference of the Methodists, turn over and receive baptism from the hands of the Methodist preachers. Once, while spending a few days at Brinkley, Ark., I was surprised to learn that some fifty young men and women who, five weeks before, were baptized after the Methodist revival, were again immersed by the Baptist ministers after their revival.

With all due respect for the hallowed customs of other religions, I must say I never enjoyed any public display equal to a "Pool-immersion" or "Camp-meeting" in Arkansas. The members themselves laugh to exhaustion seeing a white or colored Brother or Sister "ducked" in the fulvid waters, while the shouting, when the "spirit" moves, is chorussed by all the wags as well as co-religionists that surround the waters. A camp-meeting has been so often described that any effort of mine would not convey a more adequate notion of it. I will only add, that as far as "putting off the old man and vesting the new"—for moonlight recreation, frolic and fun, *Mardi Gras* and *midnight* Picnics are reticent and very restrained amusements. No wonder the poor people who are hood-winked by such religious shams are backward in social integrity. With those people religion is so superficially regarded that it is scarcely possible to make them understand why a Priest, after preaching a "stirring sermon," would not immediately baptize all who applied to him. A logical process of reasoning, and the orthodox mode of "searching the Scriptures," are lessons which heretofore they have not committed or appreciated. Still, although a thousand difficulties beset the zealous missionary in his efforts to evangelize this untutored and simple-minded people, yet I trust the day is not far distant when they shall be gathered into the "one true fold and guided by the one true Shepherd."

THE DIOCESE AND BISHOP OF LITTLE ROCK.*

As the foregoing description of "Missionary" life has been devoted to Missions in eastern Arkansas, I should consider the subject incomplete were I to omit a due reference

---

*The following are the principal towns of Arkansas, with their population in brackets, taken from census of 1880 (Rand & McNally): *Little Rock*, Capital of State [13,185], has one Catholic church (Cathedral) and a convent, conducted by the Sisters of Mercy. *Pine Bluff* [3,800]; one Catholic church and convent; Rev. J. Lucey, Pastor. *Fort Smith* [3,200]; one church and convent; Pastor, Rev. Lawrence Smith. *Helena* [3,000]; one church and convent; Pastor, Rev. J. B. Boetzkes. *Hot Springs* [4,200]; one church and convent; Pastor, Rev. P. H. Garathy.

to the Bishop and scant resources of the diocese of Little Rock.

The diocese of Little Rock, comprising the whole State of Arkansas, is subdivided into seventy-five counties, containing an area of 53,850 square miles, and a population of 802,525, of whom 591,535 are white and 210,606 colored. The country was first settled by the French in 1685; became a Territory, 1819; seceded from the Union, March 4, 1861; readmitted, 1868.

Right Rev. Andrew Byrne (consecrated March 10, 1844, died June, 1862,) was the first Bishop of the diocese. The present Bishop, Right Rev. Edward Fitzgerald, was born in the city of Limerick, Ireland, Oct. 28, 1833, and while yet a child was brought to this country by his parents in 1849. Having finished his classical course at the preparatory Seminary, Barrens, Mo., he was sent to Mt. St. Mary's, Cincinnati, and afterwards to St. Mary's, Emmetsburg, where he completed his priestly curriculum. He received Holy Orders (Aug. 22, 1857,) when he had scarcely reached the age required by the canons. He remained Pastor of St. Patrick's church, Columbus, Ohio, until he was appointed Bishop of Little Rock, Arkansas (Feb. 3, 1867). He was then supposed to be the youngest Bishop in the world.

For six years after his promotion to the Episcopate, the Catholic Directory reported for the entire diocese only an average of fourteen priests, twenty churches, and 1500 Catholics. At present, the Directory (1886) gives a list of twenty-four priests, thirty-six churches, and 8200 souls. If this extraordinary increase were the result of recent conversions from Protestantism, it would reflect on the previous administration of the Bishop, who, during the preceding fourteen years, only computed a census averaging from fifteen hundred to three thousand Catholics for the entire diocese. This increase is almost entirely due to Catholic immigration (chiefly German Catholic), which land-agents, railroad corporations, and even the secular and religious clergy have earnestly endeavored to promote. The Priests are justified encouraging immigration to several counties of middle and western Arkansas. Those who have colonized in such counties report entire satisfaction.

But from my experience of southern and eastern Arkansas, emigration would be a very unsafe risk, at least, until the Mississippi river shall be confined to its natural bed. I allow the soil is indescribably rich and fertile; but a *graveyard* and land bordering on a *slaughter-house* are also favored in this respect. I wish to adduce another fact, which no one, as far as I have seen, has hitherto stated concerning Arkansas. It is a bold and very important assumption, especially when related in the very chapter where I propose to give a synopsis of the Bishop's life.

I would state that my intercourse with the clergy of the diocese and personal experience while attending for more than four years some eight or ten counties of Arkansas, lead me to affirm that the work of converting the white or colored natives is most disheartening, if not desperate; especially those towns and districts that have facile access by railroad or steamboat. One would think that such accommodations would make the work of conversion less difficult. In mostly every other State this would be the case. I will explain the reason when I state that for almost seven years* I attended several towns in the eastern portion of the State, (Forest City, Brinkley, Palestine, DeVall's Bluff, Carlisle, and other towns,) more or less regularly, yet in all that time I did not baptize more than thirty converts. I doubt if any other missionary of the State could report greater progress. Before Father Keane's death, it was reported that he baptized one hundred converts in Pocahontas in one year. Before I question the certainty

---

* Although I devoted but four years to regular attendance of these missions, I visited several towns monthly for nearly seven years.

of this statement, it must be understood that he was then, what I was not, a resident Priest. But what gives an air of suspicion to the reported number of conversions is the subsequent fact that soon after his death church prospects in Pocahontas went down so far that the Bishop did not think it necessary to appoint a successor to Father Keane. After his death a year had scarcely elapsed, when the Bishop deemed it advisable to take down the bell of the Pocahontas church and donate it to the little new church of Brinkley, which never counted membership exceeding seventy-five.

The very fact that after twenty years only 8,200 Catholics are reported for the entire State, and that at least two-thirds of these are immigrants, clenches the truth of my assertion. When we consider that the Priests of this diocese, with the Bishop at their head, are a zealous and enlightened body of men, it is not too much to suppose that these clergymen would have made greater progress in any other State or Territory—yea, in the wilds of Africa or Cochin-China.

After fourteen years, only sixteen hundred; and after twenty years, eight thousand two hundred Catholic souls! Of the entire Catholic census I would not risk the assertion that three hundred were made converts in twenty years. Of course I make an exception of death-bed and gallows conversions, which have been very numerous in Arkansas.

Although it seems incredible, yet it is a fact, that in Tennessee, which is separated from Arkansas only by the Mississippi River, the catholic aspect and prospects are quite different. Some of the leading merchants and professional men of the State are converts to Catholicity. In the little town of Friendship, Tennessee, I remember baptizing nineteen converts in one day. In Nashville, the capital of the State, Catholicity, in worldly parlance is " *The religion.*"

In Little Rock, the capital of Arkansas, a Catholic Priest is regarded as some obsolete revivalist of the "dark ages." In Protestant sections more outlandish stories are told of the Catholic Priest and Sisterhood than ever an old Irish granny told the "rising generation" of "spooks," "ghosts" and "fairies."

What reasons can be assigned for this decadence or slow growth of Catholicity in Arkansas? The answer to this question will explain the above paradox regarding railroad and steamboat facilities being a hindrance to the growth of Catholicity in this State. Throughout all the districts that can be easily reached by cars or water, Preachers and Parsons of all denominations are in abundance. The roads generally furnish them free passes.

They hold daylight and midnight conferences and camp-meetings. I scarcely ever visited Forest City or Brinkley that some Protestant church revival was not in full glow. Distinguished preachers from Memphis, Little Rock and other less important towns were invited to fill the country pulpits. They were all sure to give the "Pope" and "Papists" a bigoted hammer before closing the Bible. Their eloquent declamations and well-rounded periods collapsed only when they had proven that the great "Book of Books" was the deadly enemy of the "Romish Church." When celebrated preachers could not be had, the blacksmith left his smithy, the farmer his steers and plow, the shoemaker abandoned material souls in his zeal to convert immortal souls. In all the towns and country villages which I had occasion to visit throughout Arkansas, I found this custom prevalent. Services were held in the churches, not only two or three times on Sunday, but invariably two or three evenings of the week. Although several of those so called "Parsons" were quite illiterate, they had a process of argument and freedom of speech that would astonish an ordinary pulpit orator. Venerable, gray-bearded old men, who happened to be a father, grandfather, brother, uncle, or cousin to half the country "folk" in the county, would take the Bible and endeavor to show his audience that the Pope was the Antichrist of the Apocalypse. The next Sunday the pulpit would be occupied by a handsome young doctor, lawyer, or bookkeeper, who would cause a dozen wagon-loads of young damsels to come and see his nice mustache, or the bisection of his hair and sandy whiskers. The following Sabbath a lady was to preach. If she could not win the hearts, she certainly gained the presence of her own sex, while it stood a question of gallantry with the other sex to hear the "lady."

To each of those little towns, the Priest could pay a hurried visit but once a month, and sometimes not once in six months. It is a great wonder that even Catholics do not lose the faith in those little towns. The society and very atmosphere they breathe appear to be opposed to the dogmatic strictness of their religion. Hence a Priest, when endeavoring to find who are the practical Catholics in the vicinage, has only to find out who abstain from meat on Fridays, and refuse to go themselves or send their children to the Protestant Sunday Schools. During the past twenty years an average of twenty Priests in Arkansas had to struggle against the prejudice ingrafted by no less than twenty thousand Preachers.

Had not God favored the Bishop of this diocese with a robust frame and unflinching perseverance, beyond a doubt the paucity of the Catholic population at present would be very discouraging. He has introduced into the diocese two or three religious Communities, who appear to be making great progress in their several missions. From my experience of the Arkansas missions, as recorded in the foregoing pages, the reader will be able to judge what this good Bishop must have suffered during the past twenty years.

Although I cannot state as a positive fact, still I always believed what an intimate friend of the Bishop once told me—that during the first three years he spent in Arkansas, he felt it necessary to carry in his vest pockets large packages of quinine while making his regular tours through the diocese, in order to anticipate or counteract the poison of *chills* and *malaria*. I remember many other privations, which, from the fact that they were more or less private, I dare not disclose. However, as the following instance does not come under the ban of secrecy, I make bold to mention it.

About seven years ago, I wrote to the Bishop, requesting him to come and dedicate a new little church that had just been erected in Forest City. As the train which left Little Rock on Saturday evening jumped the track on its way, the Bishop had to remain up all night, and only arrived in Forest City about half-past five Sunday morning. As the Bishop rapped at the door of my little sleeping compartment, rear of the church, I got up and opened the door for him. He was shivering with cold, and appeared to be very unwell. He requested me to build a fire, stating that he felt very sick. I was mortified when I had to inform him that as yet there was neither a stove nor place for a stove in the church. Although tired, and suffering intensely, the good man had no opportunity to take any refreshment until half-past one P. M., when dedication ceremony, Mass, and sermon were ended.

During many cold, and, still worse, warm nights, this veritable "Missionary" had been obliged to sleep in log-cabins and chinky mud-houses, subjected to humiliations which a layman — much less a Catholic Bishop — would feel loath to bear. His humility is noteworthy, not chiefly because, on three occasions, he positively refused a change of diocese and church preferment, but especially from his suave address and ever readiness to oblige clergy and laity who apply to him in difficulties.

Having travelled almost throughout the entire State of Arkansas, I make no hesitation in reasserting that the diocese of Little Rock is of all the Missions of the States and Territories the most arduous and unhealthy. If it were not for the annual income of "Propaganda" funds, the Priests of the diocese could not subsist. The Bishop himself once assured me that he partially supported every Priest in the State except three. Even his own revenue in Little Rock, considering that he never computed his parishioners more than a thousand, must be very limited. His Christmas "*cathedraticum*" need not incite the cupidity of robbers or burglars. Several Priests in the East and North have larger congregations than the Catholic population recorded for the entire State of Arkansas at present. Seeing this, what must be the humble condition of his life during the seven years when only fifteen hundred Catholics were reported. Until the Bishop dedicated his new cathedral (Nov. 27, 1881), during the previous fourteen years he was obliged to worship in a frame building capable of seating about five hundred people, which number he never saw in the church at one time, unless on some extraordinary occasion. His residence during all that time, and I believe to the present day, might be considered an integral part of the old church—three of the Priest's rooms being located over the right transept of the church. The inmates both "up and down" stairs had to speak in a low voice rather than be heard by people in the church, or what was more embarrassing, by colored neighbors who lived within a few feet of the *Bishop's* "*Palace.*"

Six years ago, Bishop Fitzgerald dedicated a little church in Hopefield, opposite Memphis. (Its dimensions were thirty by sixteen feet.) He delivered one of his finest lectures on the occasion. Indeed, myself and many others who could hear him through the open doors and windows, felt mortified that such beautiful thoughts, choice language and zealous efforts should be lost with luke-warm pagans and semi-civilized natives, incapable of appreciating his eloquence or estimating the spiritual import and depth of his discourse. Besides being, like his diocese, a solid "*little rock*" of authority for all knotty questions in theology, philology, and christian classics, Bishop Fitzgerald ranks amongst the best conversationalists, and is, perhaps, one of the first English scholars in the land.

Bishops in the North, East, and West, can boast of greater numbers of Priests, churches, convents, and people—in all these the present Bishop of Little Rock can make but a ludicrous comparison—but for undaunted christian zeal, humility and dignified scholarship—for power to wield the pen, or give and accept the hand of a polished gentleman—I seriously question if any individual of the American Episcopate deserves a premium before the Bishop of Little Rock. Should realities yield to my poor wishes, I would gladly say: "May this young Bishop prosper and live long enough to outnumber the average years expected in the salute, "*Ad multos annos;*" yea, may the happiness meted to him in celestial chronology be "*In aeternum coram Deo et Angelis.*"

### AN APOLOGY.

Having finished the last chapter of my little book, I would reaffirm my position regarding the Southern climate and people, especially the citizens of Memphis.

I have written things uncomplimentary to the climate of western Tennessee and eastern Arkansas. But I have stated nothing I did not believe to be true. While allowing that a poor man can make money more easily, and acquire wealth sooner in Memphis than in any other city of the United States, I must reassert what the more intelligent inhabitants themselves admit, that the climate is not the best or next best in the world. I feel convinced that if the Mississippi river were properly leveed (which work, I trust, will soon be undertaken), Memphis would be the Metropolis of the South. I hope I have said nothing to wound the feelings of any of my Catholic friends or the citizens of Memphis.

In reply to a presentation address read in my presence on the Christmas morning of '73, I stated that the words of the Irish poet, "There is no place like home," were not true in my case; "that, although Ireland was my native country, I preferred Memphis to any city in the world." I make the same declaration now. Although I have reason to regard the Priests and people of the diocese of Providence as exceedingly kind and generous, still Memphians will ever hold a first place in my fondest recollections. Were I not convinced that the climate would prove disastrous to my enfeebled health, I would sooner live in Memphis, especially among the never-to-be-forgotten parishioners of St. Bridget's, than elsewhere in the world. I have stated that I have spent nine of the best and happiest years of my life in that ill-starred city. Even now I would love to spend the evening of my life in Memphis, with the hope that my body, after death, would be deposited within the precincts of that "Mound," beside the "*remains*" of my departed comrades—the staunch and true martyr-heroes that laid down their lives for the people of Memphis.

As the facts I have recorded regarding the "Heroes" and "Heroines" of Memphis have remained in oblivion too long, I trust that, since I have endeavored to revive their saintly "memories," my critics will overlook any faults I may have committed. I also hope that Catholic papers and periodicals will afford me a kind word, seeing that I, as well as they, regret that during the past six years no one else has appropriated this most edifying and charitable subject.

D. A. Q.

www.ingramcontent.com/pod-product-compliance
Lightning Source LLC
Chambersburg PA
CBHW022021240426
43667CB00042B/1028